TRUMP

MAN

PHENOMENON

PRESIDENT

Dr. Wendell V. Fountain

authorHOUSE

AuthorHouse™
1663 Liberty Drive
Bloomington, IN 47403
www.authorhouse.com
Phone: 1 (800) 839-8640

Published by AuthorHouse 10/03/2019

ISBN: 978-1-7283-2938-3 (sc)
ISBN: 978-1-7283-2936-9 (hc)
ISBN: 978-1-7283-2937-6 (e)

Library of Congress Control Number: 2019915251

Also by Wendell V. Fountain

Clay County Country Boy

Willowbee's World

UPS and DOWNS: That's Life on Earth!

The New Emerging Credit World: Theory, Process, Practice—Cases & Application

THOUGHT PROVOKING LESSONS OF LIFE: True Short Stories

Rainbows from the Heart

How to build a Southwestern House

The Credit Union World: Theory, Process, Practice—Cases & Application

ACADEMIC SHARECROPPERS: Exploitation of Adjunct Faculty and the Higher Education System

Grace (novel, screenplay & movie)

LOVE—40 (novel & screenplay)

THE CREDIT UNION DIRECTOR: Roles, Duties, and Responsibilities

www.wendellfountain.com

*To the memory of the brilliant and courageous
Founders of this great republic and all patriotic
Americans throughout this majestic land*

Contents

Prologue

It is only fitting that I begin this book by thanking God and those great patriots before me. It was God and they who breathed life into the Bill of Rights on December 15, 1791, and the First Amendment of the Constitution which guarantees my right to free speech as cited below:

> *Congress shall make no law respecting an establishment of religion, or the prohibiting the free exercise thereof; or abridging the freedom of speech, or of the press; or the right of the people to peaceably assemble, and to petition the Government for a redress of grievances. (Compliments* of Hillsdale College).

By the time this book is in print, there will be a plethora of other books about President Donald John Trump the 45th President of the United States of America. Since I'm not an insider and/or special friend of our *phenomenal* president, I'm convinced that my perspective as an outside citizen just might make a contribution to the understanding of this man, phenomenon, and president. Though great care has been given to objectivity, it is impossible for me to separate myself from personal preference. Thus far, most of the books with which I'm familiar have been authored by close associates, colleagues, friends, television hosts, or even enemies/adversaries of the POTUS. Though I've never even had an opportunity to shake his hand, and probably never will, I often feel, think, and react as though I've known him most of my life. President Trump has a unique way of connecting with people. He is a businessman and deeply committed entrepreneur and so am I; however, I only wish I'd been one-one-thousandth as successful as he. Entrepreneurially, he has had some wins and losses. By the early 1990's, he had lost a significant amount of money, but soon bounded back. That is normal for anyone familiar with being an entrepreneur. At this point in time, I've only seen him in person once. My wife, Grace, and I waited for hours to see him at one of his early rallies in Las Vegas, Nevada February, 22, 2016 at the Southpointe Arena, which held about 8,000 people, and it was packed! Before that night, we had watched Donald Trump at every televised rally in which he participated. Many rallies we viewed online because Right Side Broadcasting Network would pan the crowds of full and overflowing event centers, while other big networks only kept the cameras trained on President Trump. To date, I have watched *every rally* he has sponsored. Early on, Fox News Corporation televised events, but soon stopped carrying Trump rallies wire-to-wire. To be generous, it could have been because others would have bellowed for equal time.

Prior to that, I/we watched him and Melania, our future and beautiful First Lady, take that famous escalator ride in Trump Tower on June 16, 2015 in which he made his stunning declaration to run for the presidency. Until then, I had essentially ignored Donald Trump. Of course, since I'm a little older than he and also very current, I knew who he was, but I never really took him seriously. In fact, I've never even watched an episode of The Apprentice, his reality TV show. From my vantage point, at the time, he was just another privileged, garash *rich guy* who had a voracious ego to feed, but that night when he declared his candidacy, things changed. What he said was a lot of what I was thinking and expressing to my friends and neighbors. It was so refreshing to see a person running for the presidency who was incredibly candid and sincere. Not since Ronald Reagan had I connected with a presidential candidate in such a way. I remember getting up from the couch, pointing at the television, and saying to my wife, "He *will* be our next president." I also knew that he would have to defeat 16 other primary challengers to win it, but I had no doubt about who the victor would be and no doubt that he would defeat Hillary Clinton, even though the Establishment on both sides of the aisle, the media, K Street, Wall Street, the Chamber of Commerce, globalists, Deep State, and others wanted nothing to change in America. It was obvious that the status quo was in *their* best interest—not that of American citizens.

President Trump and I are at opposite ends of the spectrum from a background panorama. He was born in New York City to wealthy parents, and I was born in the country into abject poverty in Doctors Inlet, Florida. Yet, he and I seem to have an implacable patriotic penchant. He nor I ever served in the military, though I tried on three separate occasions to become a member of our armed forces but was turned down because of either health or age reasons. I did, however, work for the Department of Defense for a total of 14 years as a civilian. In fact, I was one of the Secretary of Defense, Robert McNamara's, first Civilian Substitutes (CivSub) for a member of the United States Navy in 1968, serving on an admiral's staff. This program was designed to send more navy personnel to Viet Nam by replacing sea-going sailors, who were on shore duty, with civilians. President Trump, apparently, received college deferments and had bone spurs which kept him from the armed services in Viet Nam. Now, as president, he is commander-in-chief of all of our mighty military.

Ultimately, as a boy, Donald Trump became a Captain in the New York Military Academy, while as a boy, I couldn't even afford to join the Boy Scouts because we had to purchase uniforms we couldn't afford, but I still built my own little fort anyway! I watched President Trump's reaction on television, when in a processional, the New York Military Academy marched by, and I saw great pride on his face as the stars and stripes gently waved in the nightly breeze. This military school had a significant impact upon him as a youngster. It's as though the seeds of patriotism had begun to germinate. President Trump takes great pride in the flag of the United States of America. He has a love affair with our country. "America first!" He proclaims at rally after rally all over America. Many of us out here in the breadth and width of this sovereign nation have hungered for those words for decades, not because we don't care about other nations and peoples, but because we love our country first and most. Who do you love first and the most, my family or yours? America is one large family, and we must fully embrace its uniqueness, because we also must either make America great again (MAGA) and/or keep America great (KAG).

The intent of this writing is to more fully understand and appreciate President Donald Trump and what he has done and *is doing* for our home—America. I am of the opinion that only God can keep this man focused, upright, and on point, because he is and has been assailed 24/7 by the forces of evil from the very beginning. No man or woman could withstand this relentless onslaught of depravity unless there is divine support and purpose. With certitude, I am confident that believers such as Pastor Robert Jeffries of the First Baptist Church of Dallas, Texas, former Governor Mike Huckabee of Arkansas and 2016 presidential candidate, as well as the inimitable Lou Dobbs of the Fox Business Channel, among many others, concur with this muse and contemplation. Just look at the principalities and powers which have stood in staunch and defiant opposition to President Trump, but he presses on incessantly and indefatigably without regard or fear of their threats and attempts to intimidate.

Over the past couple of years or so, pundits, TV hosts, speakers, columnists, bloggers, and many others have referred to this defiance and hatred of President Trump as the Trump Derangement Syndrome (TDS), but this descriptor is inadequate, because there is something far more sinister and nefarious driving this insanity. Pure unadulterated evil is pouring over this country and the world like a mammoth bucket of black blistering tar hanging from the Moon.

Just look at the savagery in our own country and gaze upon the darkness as it creeps across our land like a deadly fungus. What about the senseless killings at the Gilroy Garlic Festival in California on a Sunday the 28th of July in 2019? Or, how about the mass murders in El Paso, Texas on Sunday August 4, 2019, which only hours later was followed up by more mass murders in Dayton, Ohio? In all of these cases, there were three different young male killers that were engulfed by darkness and evil who were armed to the teeth and lurched about with reckless abandon, shooting unarmed, innocent human beings with long guns as though they were targets at a shooting range. If this is not evil, evil does not exist. What did the leftist lunatics from the radical Democrat Party of hate do? They blamed President Trump rather than mourn for the families of those murdered by crazed Satanic killers. All of the so-called democrat candidates, screeching for the nomination of the party for the presidency, pointed fingers of blame at the president. This is what these anti-Americans do best is blame, blame, blame without even considering what can be done to prevent this insane carnage which is becoming commonplace in America. The probability that the absence of God in the public square just might have something to do with the rule of Satan in the hearts and minds of these barbarians. These are soulless creatures who roam about in search of prey just waiting for the right moment to strike, which is usually in hunting grounds called "gun free zones", because they are cowards and the only ones with guns. Liberal lunacy has created this moronic thinking, and if blame must be placed, let's lay it at the feet of delusional liberals.

Only a fool would not recognize the war on Christianity. How can anyone refute reality? There were 875 Catholic Churches in France, alone, in 2018, which were vandalized or burned by secularists and Muslims. Twelve of those churches were in Paris. The world watched the burning of the Notre Dame Cathedral on television in early 2019; even though, the powers that be did their best to convince the world that it was just an innocent accident. What about the murdering of Christians in Sri Lanka in April of 2019? That bomb blast killed 253 and wounded 500! Obviously, there *is* a war on Christianity!

Now, to the media, which has not let up with its negativity and venal attacks. Key relentless television networks and newspapers hammer away day in and day out with negative, vile, unscrupulous, vitriolic, baseless stories. CBS, ABC, NBC, MSMBC, and CNN, along with the *New York Times* and the *Washington Post* have railed against President Trump as though he is incarnate Ted Bundy, John Wayne Gacy, Jeffrey Dahmer, and Charles Manson all rolled into one. In other words, the pictures they paint are of a *monster*. They have shown complete disregard for this man as a human being and President of the United States. The so-called *free press* should have a new moniker—*rogue arbiters*. They fill their "newscasts" and "news pages", not fit for the canary's cage, with sanctimonious inuendo, jealousy, animus and enmity. The words—*they have reached a new low*—should not be uttered again, because these rogue arbiters are regurgitating salacious bottom feeders who will continue to lie and create fake news. You may be assured that this was never the intent of the Founders of this great republic who stood fast and mightily for freedom of the press and free speech.

Let's not forget the D.O.A. fraudulent Mueller Report and "investigation" which dragged on for more than two years, which was a witch hunt that cost the American taxpayer an estimated $40 million, not to mention wasted precious time, personal inconvenience, and the lives destroyed by this unbridled lawless attempt to try to find something, anything illegal that President Trump just might have even contemplated. It is and has always been about the vilification and deposing of a duly elected president. According to Robert Mueller, Special Counsel, William Barr, Attorney General, and the Deputy Attorney General, Rod Rosenstein, there was no collusion and no obstruction of justice by President Trump. Also, let's not forget who illegally and unethically appointed a conflicted Mueller in the first place—Rod Rosenstein who was acting as the Attorney General while Jeff Sessions quivered like a cowardly lion out of sight while hiding under his desk. It's incredulous that the entire "investigation" was bought and paid for by Hillary Clinton, who lost the election of 2016, but that little matter was totally ignored by Mueller and his minions. This was operation research, and in this case, manufactured "truth". In one of President Trump's tweets, he asked, "How can a republican president be charged with crimes committed by democrats?" The answer to this question is simple. The left has been taught to accuse the right of what *they* actually *do*, and since the media are, for the most part, leftists, they carry the water for the delusional Democrat Party.

Justification for the so-called investigation was all founded on an unverified and salacious Russian dossier for which a former British spy, Christopher Steele, prepared for Hillary Clinton. Then, it was embraced by a secret court called a Foreign Intelligence Surveillance Act—FISA—court which authorized the spying on of American citizens, such as Carter Page and George Papadopoulos. Americans are no longer as free as they were before September 11, 2001, and it appears we will never be again. We've allowed the politically powerful to manipulate and force citizens to surrender more and more freedom. It is still confounding that this entire political chicanery actually occurred, because everything was based on prevarications and intentional fraud. More specifically, the dossier was a document of fiction. Yet, this secret court authorized a total of four FISA warrants to spy on the Trump campaign, and the fourth FISA was signed by the acting Attorney General Rod Rosenstein. President Trump's enemies such as the socialistic/communistic Democrat Party melted down after the Mueller Report failed to support their irrational thinking and continue, frenetically, to search for another faux issue with which to harass, hammer, and harangue, President Trump, while the nation goes wanting. Their puerile and despicable behavior of stamping their little political feet is nauseous and reeks of the smell of brimstone.

From a personal perspective, it's important for me to make that delightful, joyous, and historical journey back in time to the presidential election of November 8, 2016. Remember that? That's the election Donald Trump could never win. Practically all the pollsters, apparatchiks, and CNN commentators, among many others, declared over and over that there was no way forward for Donald Trump to reach the magical number of 270 electoral votes in order to win the presidency. They were right, because he actually won 306 electoral votes! We delight in President Trump's recitation of these events at his rallies. Hillary Clinton and the status quo went down in flames! By the time the "final" numbers were tallied, it was about 2:30 a.m. Pacific Coast Time on the 9th of November, when we lived in the small Community of Desert Springs in Laughlin, Nevada. Gracie and I did what true conservatives might do. We went out into the middle of our empty, dark, dead-end street, and danced under the moonlight to this historic victory. I am confident, once again, that President Trump will be even more victorious in 2020. Now, he has an incredible, impressive, and historic record of achievements—not just promises. This also means that Gracie and I will not have to stay up into the wee hours of the morning to see the final results so that we can dance victoriously in the street.

Lastly, and most importantly, this book is about such challenging and massive real-world issues, in which President Trump is deeply committed and embroiled, as illegal immigration, health care, the economy, international trade, international relations, energy, infrastructure, the Second Amendment, the abortion industry, the Supreme Court and other federal judges, promises made, promises kept, and other great deeds, often ignored, or generally unknown by the public, for which President Trump is directly responsible.

Wendell Fountain
Surprise, Arizona

Chapter 1

Republicans and Democrats: Introduction and Context

Before the two parties can adequately be discussed relative to President Trump, it is important that an analytical vetting of the current political milieu is scrupulously and methodically examined. President Donald Trump is an unpredictable person, an enigma, who requires only about four-hours of sleep per day; yet, most us need more. In fact, his stamina is staggering. This is not new; this is how he became a very wealthy man. Anyone who has owned a business knows what it takes. You never leave the business and the business never leaves you. It takes long hours and total dedication because no one cares about your business as much as you do. As president, he begins sending out tweets often in the early hours of a day. It did not take him long to pounce upon the unique opportunity afforded him by social media and Twitter, specifically. This has become his lifeline to We the People, because the dishonest press can't filter his words and he gets to set the narrative of the day. Now, he never leaves the presidency and the presidency never leaves him. This is a true symbiotic relationship. At many of his rallies, rhetorically, he delights in joking about *now* being a politician rather than a businessman. His humor is much appreciated, but I submit that President Trump is still a businessman, running the country as he would any of his businesses. That is the crux of the matter. This is antithetical to many politicos who have lurked about in the halls of Congress for decades, while doing little to nothing and seeking reelection every two or six years. These men and women are ego-driven power-hungry political hacks. They are self-serving, duplicitous, treacherous, immoral, and often given to unethical and even illegal behavior. From President Trump's business-life, he had worked and negotiated with, for decades, some very tough business professionals, and when the contract was signed or a handshake had cemented an agreement, the deal was done and things could move forward. That does not happen in dealing with amoral politicians, because the very next day, they just might have changed their minds overnight, and the "yes" vote quickly becomes a "no" vote.

Not only are politicians untrustworthy, but bureaucrats, comprised of political appointees and civil servants who are supposed to execute the orders of the chief executive—the president—but this morass of minions often ignore or undermine directives. *One of the greatest mistakes President Trump made when he took office was not firing every Obama appointee.* To many of us who supported him, we were flabbergasted that he didn't channel "The Apprentice" and fire these treacherous people. The vast majority of them never had any intention of supporting the Trump agenda. In fact, many of them are part and parcel of the Deep State who work tirelessly to continue the work of Obama to this day. Should anyone wonder about leaks in the White House when these types of people are still employed and milling about smartly? It does not take an intellectual quotient of 160 to figure this out. There are undesirable people still embedded in the Trump administration. It's difficult to remove bureaucratic civil servants. It takes time but it can be done; however, political appointees serve at the pleasure and discretion of the chief executive, and they have no standing under the rules of the Office of Personnel Management. President Trump is a man who sees loyalty as a preeminent quality in a human being, that is, he's transactional, if you are loyal to me, then I will be loyal to you. However, loyalty is at a premium in Washington, D.C., and this is counterintuitive to him.

It is amazing how he has grown since taking office. Though transactional by nature, he has become a transformational leader and continues to perfect that leadership style. America needed a transformational leader, someone who would make unprecedented sweeping positive changes, and thank God that is the leader we elected. He is a no-nonsense, results-oriented leader. Though President Trump's enemies are legion and continue to paint verbal pictures of him being inhuman, he shows them and the world on a daily basis of his love and care for the American people and this sovereign nation in which we live. As a strong supporter of President Ronald Reagan, I never thought I would live long enough to see a president exceed President Reagan's incredible level of achievement, but President Trump has already done that in less than three years, and President Reagan was in office for a total of eight years. Returning to the growth of President Trump, he has become more of a spiritual leader than expected. He even begins each cabinet meeting with a prayer. It appears as though his relationship with and faith in God has grown. In the past two years, I have watched *every* Trump rally, and so far, he has invoked the name of God in practically all of them. When, essentially, he informally kicked off his 2020 presidential campaign in Green Bay, Wisconsin April 27, 2019, before thousands, he invoked the name of God as has become his custom. He also spoke about the $68 billion trade deficit we have with Japan and that must change. He added that Prime Minister Abe of Japan will inject $40 billion into U.S. automobile manufacturing facilities. President Trump also recognized Congressman Sean Duffy who was in attendance. He reminded viewers and attendees that Congressman Duffy was a *five-time world champion in tree climbing*—a very impressive achievement. The president is proud of his association with champions and winners. President Trump also reminded the massive throng, "We don't worship government, we worship God!" The more he speaks the more we realize just how much he is awed by many of his predecessors, the history of this country, and the humbling experience of the White House.

President Trump followed up the rally in Green Bay with another massive rally on May 8, 2019, in Panama City Beach, Florida with another great speech. The primary venue was packed by thousands, and thousands were outside. President Trump is wildly popular. This was an informative speech. The residents of the area will receive $billions in relief because of the devastation of the category five Hurricane Michael. Hud will receive $448 million to help families reestablish their housing. Because of the damage caused by Hurricane Michael, Tyndall Air Force Base was slated by the military to be closed, but President Trump intervened and the base is now being rebuilt. The base has employed 8,000 people, but from what the president said, that number will increase. He also discussed that Puerto Rico had received more financial support than any state or city in history in the amount of $91 billion! Yet, the governmental officials still criticize him for not doing enough. In addition, he spoke about the lowering of prescription drug costs, infrastructure needs, the need for tariffs on Chinese imports. The president also told the crowd about $100 million slated to curb the Red Tide which occurs frequently in Florida. The Army Corps of Engineers will soon complete their much-needed work in Lake Okeechobee. Though, the crowd heard positive things being said, with frequency, his supporters at the rally shouted, "Build the Wall!"

Republicans

The Republican Party often appears schizophrenic, that is, it's difficult to tell whether or not a conservative position or liberal madness will be present in its caucus on any given day. Over the past few decades, it has become fractious, unpredictable, and comprised of a spineless gang of careerists. The fallibility of the acronym RINO (republicans in name only) is obvious, because they are as fake as *fake news*. They should be addressed as who they are F-Rs (Fake Republicans). They are counterfeits—not the real thing. Not everyone who is a registered republican is a true conservative. In fact, even the concept of "moderate" republican is reprehensible. A moderate republican is a person who has an inaccurate intellectual, conservative, moral, and ethical compass. They defy science, because to an F-R, a woman *can be* a little bit pregnant. A female is either pregnant or not. In other words, a vote should result from conservative conviction of principle, not from what others may think should have been said or done. It's either a vote from principle or not. True conservatives do not try to explain everything away. They take a stand without fear of reprisal. President Trump does this superbly well.

If anyone in the Republican Party should be unfit to serve in our government, it is a person who lacks the ability to take an unwavering conservative position. For example, Senators, Lisa Murkowski, Susan Collins, John Thune, Ben Sasse, Lindsey Graham, and Richard Burr cannot be relied upon when it comes to conservative votes, just to mention a few, because there are a quite a number of others. Thankfully, as of 2018, we no longer have to concern ourselves with Senator Clair McCaskill of Missouri, because Joshua (Josh) Hawley dispatched her in the election. In addition, that pathetic excuse of a fake republican (F-R)—Jeff Flake of Snow Flake, Arizona—who did not even try for reelection because the people of Arizona, the state in which we live, were on to him and now he's history. What about Senator Lindsey Graham from South Carolina? It, apparently, depends on the day regarding his conservatism. One day he supports conservative positions and President Trump, the next day he sounds just like a delusional democrat. Sadly, before he passed away, Senator John McCain, without a doubt, was the king of fake republicans (F-Rs). He could never be trusted to support the Republican Party. That little game he played at the end of his life by giving a thumbs down vote which would have eliminated ObamaCare in its entirety was classic, duplicitous McCain. McCain's hatred, jealousy, and envy of President Trump he even took with him to his grave. I find that dumbfounding and unsettling, because that cannot be pleasing to God. When death is imminent, it seems to me, that forgiveness and contrition are priority number one. President Trump has said on more than one occasion that McCain's no vote has cost American taxpayers about a trillion dollars.

The greatest problem today with the Republican Party is there are entirely too many fake republicans (F-Rs) embedded in the heart of the party, especially leadership positions. The Senate Majority Leader, Mitch McConnell, is admired for the parliamentary procedural games he plays with rules of the Senate regarding such things as the 60-vote inane supermajority in the Senate in order to pass a bill. This asinine rule is not a requirement of the Constitution. It's actually a farce.[3] That's what at least two former Senate Majority Leaders—Bob Dole and Trent Lott proclaim. In 2013, former Democrat Senate Majority Leader, Harry Reid of Nevada, changed the 60-vote threshold to a simple majority of 51 votes, which opened the flood gates for the confirmation process of the Senate relative to Supreme Court nominations. As slow as Senator McConnell is, he finally learned to do that, too, regarding Supreme Court nominations after *he* became Senate Majority Leader; however, because he is a manipulative power-hungry politician, he won't do what is best for America and eliminate the need for a supermajority on other important bills. Yes, of course, Supreme Court nominations are very important, but so is every bill which reaches the Senate floor. If in a democratic-republic a majority of the vote should carry the day, then get rid of this absurd rule which renders our government hapless and feckless. Senator McConnell tolerates President Trump only because he must. It is obvious that he dislikes Trump; otherwise, why would he advise others running for political office in 2020 to run *independent* campaigns? Translated, that means distance yourself from President Trump, which is the most stupid advice you can give any republican candidate for any elective office. If I were running for any party affiliated office, I would Superglue and duct tape myself to President Trump. Fortunately, for two North Carolina GOP congressional candidates on September 10, 2019, Dan Bishop and Greg Murphy of the 9th District and 3rd District, respectively, they won their contests by ignoring McConnell's advice. The night before the election, President Trump at a rally publicly endorsed both of these men. What we do know is that before the President's endorsement, a few days earlier, Bishop was behind by 17 points and ended up winning by two points while Murphy's win was impressive. They did not distance themselves from Trump. Rush Limbaugh admonished republicans that the Republican Party was now Trump's Party and to get on board.[4] Regarding the Majority Leader, I pray that the good people of the great state of Kentucky will send Mitch McConnell back to the blue grass of his old Kentucky home in the very near future. He's done enough damage to America.

What about Paul Ryan a *cyclopean* F-R? He served in the House as Speaker for two years when the GOP was in control of the House, Senate, and the Presidency, and he couldn't deliver a thing of a conservative nature. It was obvious he despised President Trump, always pushing his *Better Way* agenda.[5] Even after President Trump was overwhelmingly elected by the voters because of the *Trump agenda*, Ryan would not let *his* "plan" go. We the People did not vote for him to be Speaker, but pathetic members of the Republican controlled House did. Even when he resigned from the Speakership, he wouldn't leave, while the lackluster republicans stood by tenuously and did nothing to remove him from the Speaker's post. If anyone should be given credit for the loss of the GOP controlled House in 2018, Paul Ryan deserves most of the credit. He is a disgrace!

When we objectively examine the nuances of the Republican Party (GOP), the name should be changed to the Compliant Old Party (COP). Republicans are not political pugilists; they'll take a dive anytime a democrat-lefty takes a swing or poke at them. They simply do not know how to fight for what is right. They fear the media like the citizens of England during the Bubonic plague (Black Death) in the summer of 1348.[6] Of course, in fairness, it is somewhat understandable, because this leftist and treacherous media pummel conservatives at will, while progressive-liberals, and now socialists, stand by with a smile and smirk on their faces, because they know they are protected. The complicit press and the electronic media will do nothing but print and say laudatory things about these haters of freedom. Though a registered republican myself, I am not faint of heart and do not have a spine of Silly Putty. All republicans need to stand tall against these anti-America Svengalis. Most republicans need to find a good orthopedic surgeon who will implant a vertical titanium rod up and down their slouching backs. Other than members of the Freedom Caucus in the House, which is supposed to be comprised of about 40 members, it is nearly the only thing the Republican Party has going for it. Of course, there are exceptions even in that caucus. True conservatives are members like the Chairman of the Freedom Caucus, Rep. Mark Meadows of North Carolina[7], who is a staunch republican, Rep. Jim Jordan of Ohio, Rep. Devin Nunes of California, Rep. Louis Gohmert of Texas, and Rep. Matt Gaetz of Florida, among others, but there are some *Never-Trumpers* in that caucus who just use it as political cover and as a resume builder, when they are in fact just another bunch of F-Rs.

President Trump is now a registered republican, but he has not always been so, according to Tom Murse in an article dated January 12, 2019.[1] In fact, Murse points out that Donald Trump has been a registered democrat who has given more money to democrats than republicans. Personally, I have never accepted the republican designation for him. President Trump is unlike the great and traditional republican Ronald Wilson Reagan who is beloved by conservative republicans and for good reason. President Trump is a populist of the people and former successful businessman who was the right person at the right time to lead America who is becoming more of a true conservative seemingly, each day, because of his battles with crazed leftists. If truth were to be spoken, both of these parties are more alike than different. Even former Governor George C. Wallace of Alabama made this prescient point in 1968 when he was running for the presidency as an independent, and I quote, "There's not a dime's worth of difference in the two parties."[2] Though,

Governor Wallace is considered to be a racist and segregationist; however, he did aptly describe the two-party conundrum of then, and I submit, there is little difference today.

What were the views of our Founding Fathers regarding political parties? Several years ago, I took a number of online courses from Hillsdale College (founded 1848) of Hillsdale, Michigan on such topics as The Federalist Papers, History 102 – American Heritage, U.S. Supreme Court, The Presidency and the Constitution, among others. Since these courses were postdoctoral, some might question why I labored over these subjects. It's really about life-long learning. Besides, for me, it had been decades since I had formerly been exposed to this type of educational experience, after all, my terminal degree is a doctorate in business administration (D.B.A.), but I found these courses to be invaluable for greater understanding about our federal government as it exists today relative to the thinking of the Founders of this great republic. In short, the Founders warned against and disliked the creation of political parties, because in their views, parties tended to divide the country rather than unite it. George Washington admonished us to avoid party politics; moreover, John Adams said, *"There is nothing which I dread so much as a division of the republic into two great parties, each arranged under its leader, and concerting measures in opposition to each other. This, in my humble apprehension, is to be dreaded as the greatest political evil under our Constitution."*[8]

The words of John Adams perfectly describe the condition of the political chaos in this country at this very moment in time. In my lifetime, which includes the era of the Viet Nam War divide of the 1960s, I have never witnessed anything like this. This all began to escalate with the duping of the American voter when they elected Barack Hussein Obama as the 44th President of the United States of America. They not only did it once but twice! The man is and was a complete fraud[9]. He was elected without portfolio. Practically everything he did was negative relative to the United States of America. This will be revisited in greater detail when the Democrat Party is discussed.

In our country, we do not need a "loyal opposition", that is, essentially, republicans and democrats. For the most part, today, that's what goes on in the British Parliament. Should we emulate the British governmental system? I think not, and that is why the Founders wanted our new government to be different. Most of them came from England where they had centuries of history; therefore, it was their intent to improve upon the ceremonial role of a monarch and the legislative Parliament. I postulate, ideally, John Adams was hoping for there to be only one party—the American Party. It Appears Adams wanted citizens to hammer out their differences to the point that only two people would be in competition for a political position, especially the presidency. Obviously, the citizens of this country spurned the warnings of the Founders, because today, we have 32 different parties, much like the multi-party system of France, with the Republican, Democrat, and Libertarian Parties, respectively, leading the way.[10] There are a multitude of reasons for this. For example, citizens have found themselves frustrated and dissatisfied with individual candidates, because they don't fit *perfectly* into their political paradigm. As a result, they foolishly create another minority party which has little to no chance of ever being accepted by the broad base of U.S. voters. This is an act of selfishness, because this is the behavior of a divider, not a uniter. This only dilutes the pool of voters, resulting in meaningless divisions. Then, there are single issue voters, such as *abortion on demand*, who are incapable of seeing the big picture, that is, voters who are myopic. Probably, the most preeminent reason is *citizen ignorance*. It has been well documented and demonstrated time and again, that the vast majority of Americans know very little about the history of their nation. How very sad. It's rare today when we can find that American history is even taught in a school. I know of a handful, but not many.

Democrats

First and foremost, everyone needs to accept the fact that the Democrat Party of 50-60 years ago was hijacked by leftists, socialists, and even Marxists a long time ago and are hellbent on undermining and destroying America by whatever means possible. The one thing these democrat misguided souls have always done so very well is to stick together. Historically, they have been monolithic until the election of 2018. When the House went back into the hands of democrats, their unity began to shake, rattle and roll, because ignorant and dangerous far-left extremists are openly challenging Nancy Pelosi's leadership as the new Speaker. Most of the kerfuffle's are coming primarily from four new radical democrat congresswomen—Alexandria-Ocasio-Cortez, Rashida Harbi Tlaib, Ilhan Omar, and Ayanna Pressley. These four female radical political terrorists, "the unmod-squad" are in constant battles with the leadership of the Democrat Party, and so far, the Speaker has done nothing about any one of them. She won't even correct them when they are obviously wrong. Nancy Pelosi clearly fears these four democrat newcomers, because she can't control them. They have become the toothpaste out of the tube. Two of these women, Tlaib and Omar, are Muslims, and at this point, it is unclear if Ocasio-Cortez has any religious preference at all; however, how can a follower of Islam, Tlaib and Omar, be allowed to serve in the Congress of the United States or even be a citizen, when the goal of Islam is to dominate the Earth with the belief and teachings of Islam and Sharia Law? Islam views all who do not believe in the teachings of Mohamed to be infidels who are to be slain. Omar, has made a number of anti-Semitic statements which, for the most part, have gone unnoticed or ignored, and there is evidence that Omar actually married her brother in order for him to become a citizen.[11] When this crop of *newcomers* is objectively examined, their American patriotism is unequivocally in question. For example, Tlaib, came into office declaring to impeach President Trump in an expletive rant unfit for a public servant. As Americans, have we fallen to this depth of darkness, mindlessness, and hatred for our president? There's nothing wrong with disagreement, but foulmouthed threats in the public arena fail the test of propriety.

For whatever reason, the media has such a steamy love affair with Ocasio-Cortez that it is nearly pornographic. Her face is omnipresent. This woman is supposed to possess an undergraduate degree in economics and international relations from Boston University.[12] As a graduate professor myself, I wonder about the educational efficacy of Boston University. How can anyone with a degree in economics come up with such a plan as the Green New Deal, which is estimated to cost the American taxpayer as much as *$100 trillion*, which includes the tearing down of *all* buildings in America, eliminating *all* air travel, and ridding ourselves of *all* cattle because they flatulate! This borders on insanity. The words which pour out of her mouth are more like word salad than intellectual discourse. She sounds unhinged. She cost New York City 25,000 new jobs and a $2.5 billion campus when she spoke out vociferously against a new Amazon headquarters relocation.[13] This woman is a young inexperienced ex-bartender, except in community organizing. Does that sound familiar?

The entire Democrat Party is rife with demented behavior. Even after the Mueller Report didn't support their narrative, they still insisted that President Trump is guilty of Russia-collusion and obstruction of justice. Before Mueller finally submitted his report, he was lauded by these people. He could do no wrong, and according to them, President Trump had better not fire Mueller, and President Trump didn't. Then, that was their position on Mueller. Now, their response since has been to accelerate their persecution of President Trump with endless subpoenas, while the country has serious issues and problems which need immediate attention from the Congress like the out of control border. Since that the Mueller madness is in the rearview mirror, the country should have moved forward, but it couldn't because of democrat refusal to accept the results of the 2016 election. Crazed delusional and mentally challenged leaders of the Democrat Party, apparently, have lost all sight of reality. Just look at the way Attorney General William Barr was mistreated and insulted when he testified before Congress on May 1st of 2019. The democrats in unison were accusing him of being a liar about the Mueller Report. It still falls into the category of momentary collective insanity. He tried to respond to questions for five hours, but that wasn't enough for them. They wanted their lawyers to question him the next day, and he said "No." My guess is he was not going to put himself through a perjury setup trap by people who had shown no respect for him or his position as attorney general. Besides, historically, it had not been done.

If it were not so serious, this would be comical. Maxine Waters as Chairperson of the Financial Services Committee, really? In April of 2019 she verbally attacked the CEOs of several major U.S. banks in a committee meeting about what they were doing to improve the situation regarding student loans. The only problem was it had been a decade or more since most of them had even offered student loans.

She is so ignorant; she doesn't even know it. Her claim to fame is shouting out before rolling cameras and sycophants, "Impeach 45!" It has been generally recognized that she is one of the most corrupt members of the Congress. She doesn't even live in the district she is supposed to serve. Rather, she resides in, reportedly, a $4 million mansion in a more upscale part of Los Angeles, California. How does a public servant, who has been on the public dole for decades afford a $4 million mansion? Should we assume, she must have asked Hillary Clinton about cattle futures? Remember when Hillary invested $1,000 in cattle futures and voilà it turned into $100,000 practically overnight?[14] Though Maxine Waters net worth is unclear, it ranges from one million to six million dollars. Regardless, of her net worth, it is inexplicable relative to her income of $174,000 per year as a democrat congresswoman, even though, she has been in Congress from 1991 to the present.

What about the morbidly obese, diminutive, Jerrold (Jerry) Nadler, democrat, who currently serves as the Chairman of the House Judiciary Committee? He is serving in his 14th term in the Congress?[15] He's another poster-person for term limits. Often, media sources take shots at President Trump for being overweight at 6'2" and 236 pounds. In a comparative sense, the rotund 5'4" Congressman Nadler, at his peak weight was 338 pounds, was extremely morbidly obese. He has had so little self-control regarding his eating habits, he had to undergo stomach surgery, even though he has deluded himself into believing that it's not his fault, it's genetics.[16] This is typical democrat behavior, blame someone or something else. It's too bad there isn't a surgical procedure which could cure him of being an irrational, delusional, democrat. If that were possible, he might become a decent congressman who represents the 10th district of New York, but then again, if term limits existed, New York City would probably have a better representative.

Let's turn our attention to another delusional democrat, Adam Schiff, Chairman of the House Intelligence Committee, what an oxymoron. "Intelligence", really? Tucker Carlson, in one of his more generous moments said, "Adam Schiff is an unbalanced hack."[17] Even citizens who are ignorant enough to watch CNN or MSNBC cannot argue that Schiff is not a polemicist. He, without one scintilla of evidence, appears before cameras practically every day and prevaricates without conscience or shame. He seems more like a cable TV contributor to MSNBC or CNN than a member of Congress. Schiff's strategy has been to dominate the "news" by maximizing his TV appearances. From January of 2017 to February 2018, he made 227 TV appearances, which totaled more than 26 hours.[18] Schiff was bankrolled by the infamous billionaire George Soros of MoveOn.org and the Open Society Foundations when Schiff's sister was married to Soros's son, Robert.[19] Anyone associated with George Soros for any reason, in whatever manner, should be looked upon with a trepidatious jaundiced eye. It is common knowledge that George Soros, over several decades, has financially wrecked and ruined many *countries* for his own self-aggrandizement.

The current Speaker of the House, Nancy Pelosi, will do just about anything to have that gavel in her hand. She is highly motivated by power. Just before the election of 2018, she had to agree to abdicate the Speakership in 2022 just to get a "deal" among democrats who wanted someone younger than a 78-year-old as Speaker.[20] Ten years ago, she showed her lack of intellectual acuity when she was Speaker during the ObamaCare debacle—The Patient Protection Affordable Care Act of 2010. The bill was approximately 2,300 pages, and the members of the House had about 24 hours in which to read it. Even if they had the inclination to do it, that feat was nearly impossible. Reading is one thing but comprehension is quite another. We can safely say that it is highly probable that no one in Congress actually even read it; however, Nancy Pelosi didn't see this as an issue. She had a solution to the problem. As she explained, "We have to pass the bill so that you can find out what is in it, away from the fog of controversy."[21] As the author of this book, I ask anyone who reads this, "Isn't this one of the most idiotic, ignorant, and stupid statements for the Speaker of *our* House to ever utter?" If this line of thinking is to be followed, why should any bill ever be read? Just pass it and find out what happens, and she considers herself to be a leader? I would relish the idea of *her* giving *me* a blank check just to find out how much for which I would write it. Since she is supposedly worth in excess of $120 million, you may be assured that the amount would be at least eight digits. With some frequency, I do see clips of her on news shows prattling on about how much President Trump lies. She has even said that about the Attorney General William Barr.

She, and other democrats constantly criticize and accuse President Trump and Attorney General Barr of lying. In fact, Nancy Pelosi accused General Barr of lying to Congress. The plan was to hold him in contempt of Congress. Congress held the former Attorney General, Eric Holder, in contempt and nothing happened, but then he was a democrat, wasn't he?

Until now, only a select few members of the House of Representatives have been discussed, but the Senate is filled with vile, venal, and vacuous arbiters of vitriol and hate. First-up is Senator Dianne Feinstein who resides in her $16.5 million Pacific Heights mansion of San Francisco, California. Of course, she lives far from the hypodermic needle and human feces pandemic created by illegal invaders, drug addicts, mentally disturbed, and homeless people. I haven't been to the city by the bay for about 20 years, and it's probable I will never visit that city again. I refuse to even temporarily reside in filth and squalor. If anyone watched her "performance" during the Judge Brett Kavanaugh confirmation hearing, there should be no doubt about her hypocrisy and deceitfulness. Her unethical behavior should have been called out at the time, but eunuch republicans just sat their sputtering like old Model-T-Fords, probably because so many of them still remember those old cars first-hand, including democrat Diane Feinstein. After all, she was born in 1933 and is 86 years old and today is a very wealthy woman.[22] She is another representative who clearly demonstrates why term limits are about the only way to jettison these disingenuous characters; however, the possession of power, once gained, has an attraction more powerful than being hooked on Chinese Fentanyl.

During the Kavanaugh hearing, she was asked if she were responsible for the leaking of sensitive classified information, and she just sat there, stumbling over her words, and looking over to her staff for a response. She even asked *them* if she had leaked anything. Of course, with incredulity, they told her that she had not done that. Her response, then, was that no leak came from her office. She has constantly accused President Trump of collusion with Russia, while knowing full well that was unfounded total nonsense. She was the ranking member of the Senate Intelligence Committee and knew better. She was hip-deep in the conspiracy to overthrow our duly elected president, resulting from her association with Fusion GPS and ex-British spy Christopher Steele who supplied manufactured superfluous "dirt" in a fictional dossier, funded by Hillary Clinton, on Donald Trump. This was initiated by Daniel Jones, one of her former staffers.[23]

In August of 2018, Bre Payton of *The Federalist* wrote an article in which she reported that Senator Feinstein's personal driver for 20 years was a Chinese Spy. Interestingly, the FBI had shown up at Feinstein's office five-years prior and disclosed that her driver was a mole. At that time, Feinstein was serving as Chairwoman of the Senate Intelligence Committee who obviously had access to classified information. Finally, she dismissed her driver and never even mentioned it to her staff.[24]

Curiously, 26-year-old Bre Payton, who reported this story in *The Federalist* passed away 147 days after Bre's article was published. This is not an attempt to create a conspiracy narrative, but what is the serendipitous probability of a youthful Bre Payton passing away in a rather short period of time after the publication of her article because of H1N1 (Swine) flu plus a possible complication of meningitis? It seems to me, that an autopsy was in order, because just guessing at her cause of death is unacceptable. The Mayo Clinic has stated that this flu is fatal in rare cases.[25] Some of us are still stymied by the mysterious death of Chief Justice Antonin Scalia, in which an autopsy was not performed either.

From a personal point of view, I always enjoyed Bre Payton's succinct and insightful commentary on TV regarding her work and research. She is and has been missed. May God bless Bre, her family, colleagues, and friends. Though she no longer walks among us, she is not forgotten.

Another delusional democrat female who spews fire, lava, and brimstone like the Kilauea Volcano of the Big Island of Hawaii regarding President Trump and Attorney General William Barr is the junior Senator Mazie Keiko Hirono of Hawaii. She was born to an American mother in Fukushima Prefecture, Japan in 1947. Hirono became a naturalized citizen in 1959, the same year Hawaii became America's 50th state. She is America's first Buddhist senator. It appears the family struggled financially in Hawaii, they had little money; however, she was still able to graduate from the University of Hawaii at Manoa with a B.A. degree and followed that up with a law degree from Georgetown University.[26] It's amazing how impoverished people can graduate from a prestigious university of the caliber of Georgetown, but then, she was a double minority, a woman of Asian descent. Affirmative Action at its finest.

A quick review of her "work" history is quite lacking. For the most part, she has held just one political position after another. Stated differently, it appears that she has been on the public dole most of her adult life and a political hack, at least from 1981 to the present. She was reared in Honolulu. Does that remind you of anyone? Her behavior in the AG Barr hearing of May 1, 2019 was absolutely reprehensible. She and others actually called Barr a liar and that he was the attorney for President Trump, rather than the attorney general of the United States. Even if she believed it, that was not a professional manner in which to make inquiry. As I watched the hearing, all of the democrats on the committee behaved like lobe-toothed piranha, trying to devour Barr alive.

In summary, since this book is about President Trump, the man, phenomenon, and president, it is important to glean an understanding of the types, kinds, and behaviors of the people with whom he must relate on a regular basis. Those who were selected are but a handful of rabid and sordid elected officials who are clearly confused, conflicted, and ruthless. A quick review of the information provided, clearly demonstrates that he has enemies on both sides of the aisle; albeit, primarily on the democrat side—not to even mention an all-out assault by the so-called main stream media. Unquestionably, the Democrat Party as a whole has never accepted the results of the 2016 presidential election and have sat about to rectify, in their eyes, the election of President Donald Trump by whatever legal or illegal methodologies required for the purpose of accomplishing that goal. In general, the leftist delusional democrat mob will stop at nothing.

Now, regarding the nation's problems and the Trump agenda. The top issue for America is *immigration* which is discussed in chapter two.

———

Endnotes

1   https://www.thoughtco.com/was-donald-trump-a-democrat-3367571.
2   The author was in attendance at a speech Governor Wallace delivered in 1968 at the Jacksonville Coliseum in Jacksonville, Florida for the purpose of a college speech class.
3   Former Senate Majority Leaders: 60-Vote Threshold is a 'Farce' reported by Leah Barkoukis of Townhall.com, April 6, 2017.
4   Garcia, Victor – Fox News – https://www.foxnews.com/politics/rush-limbaugh-republicans-trumps-party–get-on-board (April 2019).
5   USNews – (9-7-2016) https://www.usnews.com/opinion-intelligence/articles/2017-03-27/paul-ryan-has...
6   History.com Editors, updated 4-15-2019, Black Death – https://www.history.com/topics/middle-ages/black-death.
7   Boyle, Matthew (January 28, 2019) https://www.breitbart.com/politics/2019/01/28/mark-meadows-re-elected-chairman-of hou...
8   Howell, Derek (January 17, 2014) FREEDOM OUTPOST, https://freedomoutpost.com/founding-fathers-loathed-political-parties/
9   McCarthy, Andrew (November 9, 2013) National Review Obama's Massive
10 Fraud/http://nationalreview.com/2013/11/obamas-massive-fraud-andrew-c-mccarthy/List of political parties in the United States – (May 2018) https://ballotpedia.org/List_of_political_parties_in_the_United_States.
11 Bauman, Christine (October 24, 2018) New Evidence Supports Claims That Ilhan Omar Married Her Brother, Alpha News. https://alphanewsmn.com/new-Evidence-supports-claims-that-ilhan-omar-married-her-brot...
12 Life, Education & Platform – Biography – https://biography.com/political-figure/Alexandria-ocasio-cortez.
13 Dibble, Madison – Thanks to AOC and Her Fellow Democrats, Amazon Just Pulled the Plug on Their NYC Headquarters – https://

ijr.com/thanks-to-aoc-and-her-fellow-democrats-amazon-ditched-nyc-hq/

14 How Hillary Made That $100k in Cattle Futures, https://www.barnhardt.biz/2013/08/09/how-hillary-made-that-100k-in-cattle-futures/

15 Wikipedia – Jerry Nadler – https://en.wikipedia.orgwiki/Jerry_Nadler

16 Congressman Jerry Nadler – Nadler, as a Last Resort, Sheds Weight by Surgery https://www.jerrynadler-com/news-clips/nadler-last-resort-sheds-weight-surgery.

17 American Boomer Daily – https://www.washingtontimes.com/news/2018/feb/27/inside-beltway-adam-schiff-strategy-...

18 Inside the Beltway: Adam Schiff's strategy includes the power of 227 TV Appearances-...-https://www.washingtontimes.com/news/2018/feb/27

19 Rep. Adam Schiff's Shocking Ties To George Soros Revealed/ https://conservative-post.com/rep-adam-schiffs-shocking-ties-to-george-soros-revealed/

20 Zanotti, Emily (December 13, 2018) of the Daily Wire – https://www.dailywire.com/news/39329/Nancy-pelosi-inks-deal-stay-speaker-%E2%80%/94-...

21 Christopher, Tommy (November 17, 2013) https://www.mediate.com/tv/the-Context-behind-nancy-pelosis-famous-we-have-to-pass-the...

22 Dianne Feinstein Biograph – https://marriedbiograph.com/dianne-feinstein-Biography/

23 Payton, Bre (August 3, 2018) The Federalist-https://thefederalist.com/2018/08/03/sen-dianne-feinsteins-personal-driver-20-years-chinese...

24 Ibid.

25 Faulkner, Trisha (December 29, 2018) INQUISITR, https://www.inquisitr.com/ 5226976/bre-paytons-cause-of-death-flu/

26 Mazie Hirono – Wikipedia – https://en.wikipedia.org/wiki/Mazie_Hirono.

Chapter 2

Immigration: Legal and Illegal

The issue of immigration has become one of the most important and controversial issues, benefits, and threats to American society. It is not about preventing peoples from foreign nations from becoming naturalized American citizens. It is about those people becoming Americans. Contrary to what some people claim, there is an American culture held together by a common language—English. What has been going on in this regard for many decades is that America is becoming Europe, that is, many different languages are being spoken in this country rather than English. America used to be referred to as the "melting pot", but that is no longer what's transpiring. We have become a "salad bowl." The carrots want to remain carrots and the tomatoes want to stay tomatoes and so forth. Businesses, local, state, and federal government even print and record information in different languages, especially Spanish—press 1 for English and press 2 for Spanish. Is it any wonder why immigrants do not become proficient in English? Another reason this is important is because English is the language of commerce around the world.

If we would respect the lessons of history, immigrants who could not speak English came to this country legally by the millions to become Americans. According to the Library of Congress, more than 15 million immigrants came to America between 1900 and 1915, which was about equal to the amount of the previous 40 years.[1] Italians, Germans, Hungarians, Russians, citizens of Scandinavian countries, among others, came through Ellis Island in New York to be Americans. They did not come here seeking handouts, they only wanted a hand up and an opportunity to pursue their American dream. It was not uncommon for immigrants to only speak English in their homes, because they wanted to be like all other Americans. They didn't abandon their language or heritage, but they wanted to be fully integrated into the American culture and learning English was pivotal.

Since our country has degraded into chaos regarding legal and illegal immigration, it's time that serious consideration be given to suspending *all* immigration for at least a decade. No one should become an American citizen during this period. This might sound draconian, and it is, but we need to know who is here and why they are here. We need to know just how many legitimate citizens reside in America. If Immigration and Customs Enforcement (ICE) agents should knock on my door to question me about who I am and why I'm here, I have no problem, because I have nothing to hide. I've been a citizen from birth. Only people who have something to conceal are more apt to resent and reject the inquiry of government agents. This is America and only American citizens should be permanent residents. This has nothing to do with discrimination or xenophobia. It is about ensuring the sovereignty, safety, and national security of this country. Typically, on an annual basis, 600,000 to 1,000,000 immigrants become citizens of the United States. Historically, citizens from Mexico lead among other countries in the naturalization process.[2]

This book could easily be bogged down in pieces of legislation which do not and cannot resolve the current immigration issues of today, because the United States Congress is and has become inert and fatuitous. This is not just an indictment of Congresses for the past few years, because essentially Congress has been absent without leave from the immigration legislative process for decades. Even though, research indicates people can legally immigrate into the U.S. in as little time as eight months and as long as two years,[3] that is not generally true. Though anecdotal, many who want to become citizens must wait 10-15 years and spend a lot of money in the process. Obviously, this is unacceptable. The excessive time issue is motivation for people to come into the U.S. illegally. After all, of the approximately 2,000 miles of our southern border, much of it is wide open. If we had a substantial wall or barrier where needed, illegal immigration and invasions of people from other countries would soon cease to exist. Walls/barriers work. There are many countries around the globe which rely heavily on them. Democrats are such hypocrites. They are the ones as a monolith who have fought tooth and nail to prevent the building of a wall/barrier on the southern border; however, they insist that a wall be erected around their convention center in Milwaukee, Wisconsin for the 2020 Democrat Convention. Pathetic!

For a better understanding of immigration, we need to examine the recent and more extended past. First, the 13th Amendment abolished slavery; therefore, slaves became citizens. Second, it is important to comprehend why the 14th Amendment to the Constitution came into being. Regardless of what ignorant and unlearned people say, that amendment was to provide citizenship for children of those former slaves. Section I of this amendment has been interpreted to mean that any child born on U.S. soil automatically becomes a citizen. That is nonsense. Birthright citizenship should never have happened and now that it has, it should be ended.[4] Only *citizens* born in America and *naturalized* citizens can bestow citizenship onto their progeny. President Trump is right about the manipulation and bastardization of the Constitution. If We the People had a Congress with integrity, principle, and decency, this could be resolved in less than an hour, but we don't. We haven't had a responsible Congress in decades. As President Trump often says, "All talk and no action." Somehow, someway, we must limit the terms of these governmental self-serving parasites. For example, just as a suggestion, eight years (four terms) in the House and 12 years (two terms) in the Senate is enough and no retirement plans and no free medical care. The Founders never intended that service to the country be a career. If the presidency has a limit of two four-year terms, then all other elective offices should have term limits. This is just common sense and logic.

In more recent times, immigration law has resulted in some interesting changes and challenges. For example, in 1952 the Immigration and Nationality Act (McCarran-Walter Act) actually determined quotas for skills needed in our country.[5] This is not unlike what other countries require. It is what is meant by President Trump when he talks about those who enter America should enter through merit. America does not need an unlimited supply of low-skilled workers. We need men and women who are skilled, highly skilled, love America, and are thankful and proud of this great sovereign nation. Put another way, they bring benefit rather than liability.

A year later (1953), in the Supreme Court case of Kwong Hai Chew v. Colding, 344 U.S. 590, the Supreme Court determined, "The

Bill of Rights is a futile authority for the alien seeking admission for the first time to these shores. But while an alien lawfully enters and resides in this country, he becomes invested with the rights guaranteed by the Constitution to all people within our borders."[6] The operative word is *lawfully*. Simply put, if a person is in the U.S. legally, they have the protections of the Constitution. This case made it clear that illegal aliens have no standing in this country.

In 1954, President Dwight David "Ike" Eisenhower initiated "Operation Wetback" as a repatriation project of the United States. The plan was aimed at illegal Mexican immigrants who worked for low wages for U.S. farmers. Though accurate numbers are in dispute, estimates of 1,300,000 were forced to leave, "and local INS officials claimed that an additional 500,000 to 700,000 had fled to Mexico before the campaign began."[7] Ike had more than a casual knowledge of the southwest. He was born in Denison, Texas in 1890 and soon moved to Abilene, Kansas where he grew up. After graduating West Point, he was stationed in San Antonio, Texas as a second lieutenant where he met his wife to be—Mamie Geneva Doud in 1915 and they later married in 1916.[8] It has been suggested by some that this initiative occurred because of President Eisenhower's concern for returning WW II veterans regarding viable employment opportunities. Of course, though speculation, farmers would have had to pay more for labor, but it would seem that a veteran would rather work in the hot fields than be shot at by the enemy.

In 1965, the Democrat Party's passage of the Immigration and Naturalization Act (Hart-Celler Act) dealt a deadly blow to the cultural makeup of America. Much of what went into this piece of legislation was a kneejerk reaction to the civil rights movement. Politicians are usually reactive, but seldom proactive.

> *All told, in the three decades following passage of the Immigration and Naturalization Act of 1965, more than 18 million legal immigrants entered into the United States, more than three times the number admitted over the preceding 30 years. . . . By the end of the 20th century, the policies put into effect . . . had greatly changed the face of the American population.*[9]

Yet, the pompous prevaricating President Lyndon Baines Johnson said that this was not revolutionary and would have no impact on our daily lives or add to our wealth or power.[10] It was delusional democrats like megalomaniac Johnson and "tanked Teddy" Kennedy, who rammed this horrible piece of legislation through. They have injured this great nation in multifarious ways. Ted Kennedy was a coward and drunk who let 28-year-old Mary Jo Kopechne, supposedly, drown in about five-feet of water on Chappaquiddick Island of Edgartown, Massachusetts on July 18th of 1969, after he ran off the little bridge over the pond in his Oldsmobile. If Neil Armstrong had not been the first man on the moon on July 20, 1969, Kennedy would not have had such an easy time of it with the press, but Armstrong's fantastic achievement blanketed the news. Johnson's War on Poverty was a bust and has cost this nation trillions of dollars and solved nothing. He escalated the Viet Nam War to beyond belief. At the height of the war, we had 500,000 troops on the ground, while he tried to play the role of a commanding general who waged the war from the White House.

This 1965 immigration law ensured family reunification, eliminated national-origin quotas, and catered to people from Asia, Africa, and Latin America, rather than Europe, while setting quotas for the West. This law is the big hook to chain migration, and chain migration is wrapped around the throat of America. This is the issue with which president Trump is having to contend. He wants to end chain migration. It makes no sense that the entry of one person could bring an additional 20 or more, just because the citizen is related to others from their previous home country.

There has been no attempt to recount all of the immigration laws, court cases, or executive actions therewith; however, most legislative actions have been deleterious to the prosperity of America. There are very few politicians who are members of Mensa. Most of them have never done a decent day's work and have no idea how to go about it. This is why it is easy to assert that President Donald Trump is not a politician. Even though he was born into wealth, and now President of the United States, his father Fred Trump taught him the value of frugality and the dignity of work. Young Donald Trump worked long hours on construction/development sites, proving himself. He worked alongside others in the construction and building trades to learn the business. To this day, his vernacular and much of his overt behavior reflects his association with the common man, the typical American male, and that's one of the reasons he is a beloved president and human being.

At this juncture, there is one more crucial immigration law to be discussed, and that is the Immigration and Reform Act of 1986 (aka Simpson-Mazzoli Act). This was signed into law by President Ronald Reagan in his second term. Before the specific provisions contained in this law are enumerated, background information and context need to be provided. Those of us who were around in 1986 really know the backstory, which is seldom presented in formal settings or published documentation. As a national figure and radio host, Rush Limbaugh has done his best to not let the truth be forgotten. He reminds his audience of about 20 million listeners on a regular basis of the deceit of the democrats in 1986. From 1977-1987, the Speaker of the House was Thomas Phillip "Tip" O'Neil a democrat from Massachusetts.[11] Publicly, Tip O'Neil was very critical of President Reagan. On a number of occasions, he stated, in so many words, that Reagan was intellectually challenged. He insulted Reagan with some frequency; yet, he had a somewhat cordial relationship "after hours". They often met at the end of a day to discuss problematic bills and the Immigration Reform and Control Act was one of them. In the final analysis, Tip and the democrats snookered President Reagan and the compliant republicans by promising that they would provide better border security at a later date if 2.7 million illegal Mexicans were granted amnesty first.[12] They agreed, and the democrats reneged and did not provide funding for more border patrol personnel and other security measures. Simply put, Tip and the democrat-controlled House lied, which is why the delusional democrats of today cannot be trusted. President Trump is aware of this duplicity and that's one of the reasons he has found other ways to get funding for the wall.

Specific provisions of the Immigration Reform and Control Act of 1986 include: sanctioning employers for hiring illegal aliens, providing amnesty to illegal aliens who have been residing in the U.S. since 1982, increased enforcement of the border, and it also criminalized the hiring of an illegal immigrant.[13] These provisions, on the surface, appear to really solve the immigration enigmatic conundrum, but the law must be enforced, and it has been ignored.

President Trump is aware of this situation, and that's one of the reasons he has sought other sources of funding for the border wall. Besides, their hatred of the president, because of his success, has them blinded to what is best for the American people. They cannot or will not allow the president to have a "win" with funds for the essential border wall. These delusional democrat cretins actually think they might have a chance of defeating the greatest president of our lifetime in 2020. That will not happen!

Southern Border on Fire

Despite what the radical delusional democrats maintain, what's going on at the southern border of the United States is unprecedented. Historically, we have never seen anything like this. It's aflame with illegal activity. The Mexican drug cartels are dictating the terms and conditions from the Mexican side in collaboration with despicable and traitorous American officials and agents on the U.S. side. The radical democrats won't even concede that it's at least a crisis. It causes one to ponder upon what planet these people reside. These elected officials are practicing malfeasance while holding office. It causes one to wonder if these politicos ever watch a TV show which underscores the immigration crisis, but also the humanitarian crisis which has become catastrophic. Thousands of immigrants are being housed in spaces built for hundreds, while thousands more are on their way. Many of these invaders have discovered that as a family unit, they will be allowed to cross the border into the U.S. As a result, they have formed "temporary" family units which includes the renting of children. Later the "rented" children go back across the border so that they can be rented again.

Based on the current apprehension of illegals at the border, that number will likely eclipse 1,000,000 arrests in 2019. This country has never experienced such an exponential explosion. Most of these arrests are not happening at the ports of entry along the border, because hundreds of miles of the border have little to no impediment to ingress into the U.S. Why would a criminal/illegal person risk the presenting of themselves at a port of entry? These are devious and malevolent humanoids without a conscience.

This is a much more serious of a problem today than it was in 1986. Then, it was mostly Mexicans illegally crossing. Now, there are people crossing the border illegally from countries around the world. In addition, some of the worst people known to man are pouring over the border unimpeded. Jihadists, ISIS, MS-13 gang members, Zeta gang members, and other killers and murderers are finding their way into the U.S. through shrewd and cunning machinations. As of February 2019, a National Emergency on the southern border, declared by President Trump, exists and the radical democrats do nothing but try to stop the president from securing it. Who does this party represent? Combined, the U.S. is being invaded by tens of thousands from the southern triangle countries—Guatemala, Honduras, and El Salvador; Moreover, if the immigration laws are not drastically overhauled soon, there is a potential for millions to illegally enter the U.S. without consequence. These people crashed through the southern border of Mexico with relative ease and marched through Mexico, once again, with very little opposition. Not only were they, for the most part, unimpeded, the "caravans" were organized, supported, and assisted with various forms of transportation to reach the U.S. border so that the border patrol and immigration officials would be overwhelmed. This follows the Cloward-Piven strategy[14] and the teachings of their mentor Saul Alinsky who authored the book *Rules for Radicals*,[15] and that is undeniable. Cloward-Piven taught insurrectionists how to defeat social systems, and the overwhelming of the immigration system was the key to destroying it. Though it is speculation, this recent initiative of creating caravans of citizens from other countries has leftist fingerprints all over it. This is at the root of why the Democrat Party does not want a wall. If a wall/barrier was in place all along the southern border where needed, there would be no crisis at the border. President Trump put this as a central agenda item at the beginning of his candidacy for the presidency, because at every rally held, his supporters chanted over and over again, "Build the wall! Build the wall! Build the wall!"

The wall is not just about illegals entering the U.S., it is also about preventing sex trafficking and human smuggling, kidnapping of adults and children, and stopping the free flow of deadly drugs which come over the U.S. border on a daily basis. It is difficult to accept that the Speaker of the House, Nancy Pelosi, actually declared, "We're not doing a wall. . . . So that's that. . . . No, it has nothing to do with politics, it has to do with a wall is an immorality between countries; it's an old way of thinking."[16] How can an informed, intelligent person make such an ignorant statement? Keeping that fatuous statement in mind, it was reported that, "Two-thirds of migrants traveling through Mexico [to U.S. border] report experiencing violence during their journey, including abduction, theft, extortion, torture, and rape, according to Doctors Without Borders MSF) . . .. Almost 1 in 3 women surveyed by MSF said that had been sexually abused during their journey—60 percent through rape."[17]

It's clear that Mexican drug cartels also indulge in the business of sex trafficking. "Narco gangs, including Zetas, have diversified their portfolio to include buying and selling women as slaves."[18] To further explore this horrible practice, one young woman told her story about being deceived, at the age of 16, regarding her unfortunate circumstances. She was held under duress in a hotel room where she was forced to have sex with as many as 40 men per day.[19] Obviously, sexual trafficking is a huge problem. "The U.S. Department of State estimates that as many as 20,000 young women and children are trafficked across the border from Mexico each year. . .. [And] between 400 and 500 people are known to die while attempting to cross the border between Mexico and the United States."[20] This is despicable and unacceptable. We must rid ourselves of magnets which draw vulnerable people to try to illegally enter the U.S. Most of these people are in search of free money, free housing, free medical, free education, free food, and the promise of a good job. The American taxpayer should not have to bear this burden. After all, these people come into this country by breaking the law. They are here illegally; therefore, they do not have Constitutional protections, and even if they did, taxpayers don't expect and do not get free things. We are a capitalist country, and as President Trump often says, "We will never be a socialist country."

What about the Sinaloa and other Mexican cartel primary business—illegal drugs? Drugs are pouring over the southern border at will. The drug cartels control both sides of the border. It has become common knowledge that approximately 70,000 U.S. citizens annually die from drug overdoses, and it's not because the federal budget is insufficient, because the budget increased from $23.8 billion in 2013 to more than $27.7 billion in 2018.[21] Clearly, funding is not the issue, but a wall/barrier at the southern border will help immensely in impeding the flow of drugs. It is ironic and sad that teenagers in Washington, DC have serious drug use problems. When compared to the states of Rhode Island, Vermont, and Oregon, respectively, DC comes in fourth.[22] It would be naïve to assume that a wall/barrier would completely eliminate the entry of illegal drugs into the U.S., but it is a significant step in the right direction. Teenagers and adults would benefit from slowing or stopping the flow.

The issue is really the ease of entry into the U.S. from Mexico. To illustrate this point, I recall doing a training session in San Diego in 1987 in which after the seminar was concluded, we were provided with a bus which accommodated about 30-40 of us and we all went into Tijuana, Mexico as tourists. A young Mexican woman served as our guide. We spent several hours visiting cantinas, shops, and typical tourist traps. Late that afternoon, we headed back. About a mile before we crossed the border, I looked out of the right side of the bus window and noticed, on a high hill next to the road, that it was crawling with people. I could even see vendor carts being pushed up the high incline. I flagged down our guide on the bus and asked about the vendor carts and all the people on the hill. She explained to me that the carts were there so that the people could get something to eat before they crossed the border after dark. She further explained that this was usually done on a daily basis. Even back then, Mexicans flowed freely into the U.S. without consequence.

In late January of 2019, Customs and Border Protection of the U.S. made a massive seizure of fentanyl which is 100 times more powerful than morphine at the Nogales point of entry. It weighed about 254 pounds and came in powder and pill form with a value of approximately $3.5 million. It had been hidden in a compartment with a false bottom of a tractor-trailer which hauled produce. In total, about 650 pounds of illegal drugs were removed.[23] When I saw this on the news, I really found this to be ironic, because in 2016, I was doing research for a novel about a truck driver who hauled produce with his tractor-trailer and this was one of the ways drugs could be transported into the U.S. My research also uncovered far more sophisticated ways and means of drug trafficking.

The author of the article which chronicled this story made an erroneous conclusion, because she took the wrong position. She concluded that there was really no need for a fence or wall, because the authorities were catching these criminals at ports of entry. To some degree, that is correct, but what about the hundreds of miles of border where illegal drugs are being brought into the U.S.? The truth is, if drugs are being discovered at ports of entry, can you imagine how many drugs are not being interdicted in other wide-open areas of the border? Build the wall!

According to Josh Stevens of Leap Frog America (politics), he identified eight (8) challenges which he learned about when he toured 171 miles of border in Texas in May of 2019.[24] (1) Cartel Control – the violent del Noreste, (2) Proximity to Population – closeness of the border to American residences, shopping centers, and even schools, (3) Where the Cane Grows High – Carrizo cane is dense, tall, and spreads fast along the Rio Grande, (4) Lack of Resources – not enough lighting stands and electronic surveillance equipment, (5) Two Bridges – these physical structures at Laredo connect the state of Texas to Nuevo Laredo in Mexico, (6) Sea of 18-Wheelers – it is common for these tractor-trailers to contain illegal immigrants, (7) Disadvantaged in Vehicles – the paucity of navigable roads, and (8) – Questionable Families – the creation of faux families is common by men, women, and children.

It is important to note, as described above, that these problems exist in obvious areas along the border, but what about the hundreds of miles separating the U.S. with Mexico where the border has no wall or even a fence? Illegal activity has little to no bounds. Illegal immigrants/invaders have few impediments which prevent them from crossing into the U.S. American citizens along the border are no longer willing to wait for the U.S. government to do their job by building an appropriate wall/barrier. As an example, Kris Kobach, former Secretary of State of Kansas, has been leading the fight for citizens to build the wall. Through a GoFundMe account, a critical half-mile stretch of border wall was erected in El Paso, Texas. Kobach and others asked for permission from landowners to build this strategic section because illegal drugs and immigrants cross into the U.S. routinely. Kobach showed off this barrier over the 2019 Memorial Day weekend.[25] Of course, the democrat government of Sunland Park, where the project ended, objected because it claimed that proper permissions had not been obtained from them. Radical and delusional democrats do everything they can to injure America.

This bunch of foolhardy miscreants are mimicking the behavior of mindless liberal federal judges who perch high up in San Francisco, California like birds of prey. Rather than mindless liberal minions of the court ordering our lives, let's look at the appropriate steps which should be taken to secure the border.

One-hire at least two new well-qualified border patrol agents for each of the approximately 700 miles where the U.S. is most vulnerable—1400-1500 posthaste.

Two-require all of the agents to stop *everyone* who attempts to cross the border, by whatever means necessary, which includes force. New rules of engagement must be put into place. No more diaper changing. This is absurd!

Three-no border patrol agent, for any reason, should ever leave their post until relieved by another agent.

Four-increase early electronic notification technology for all of the nearly 2,000 miles of the border, including agent communications among and between each other.

Five-when regular military or national guard personnel are used to support the border patrol agents, grant them the authority to do whatever is necessary to repel invaders. These men and women are supposed to be a fighting force. They are not babysitters. The Posse Comitatus Act does not apply despite ignorant liberal drivel. The Army is being used to repel invaders; the Army is not being used against the American people.

Six-anyone associated with the Obama administration should be fired and replaced with patriotic Americans who will secure our border. If their jobs fall within the purview of civil service regulations, they should be reassigned to other duties with no loss of pay or seniority.

Seven-appoint a highly skilled and capable patriot to serve as the Secretary of Homeland Security. President Trump's nomination of

Kevin Mcleenan, as *acting* Secretary of Homeland Security, is not the best choice. Many of his advisers have a kinship with the swamp and Deep State and have ill-advised President Trump. Mcleenan is the wrong person. Once again, anyone associated with the Obama administration is more than likely not the right individual. He's already been, according to him, overwhelmed with the border crisis. America needs an innovative thinker with Avant-garde solutions, not I need help, while sucking his thumb and hiding from sight. What's wrong with putting Tom Homan, former Director of ICE, into that position? He's a man with passion, border solutions, and fully supports the president.

Eight-anytime a delusional democrat federal judge puts up a roadblock, do all that's humanly possible to expeditiously get that decision before the Supreme Court for a ruling.

Nine-encourage *private sources and organizations* to help pay for the wall, while using all federal funds available for its construction. Thus far, the Trump administration has been doing a good job with finding pockets of federal dollars for the construction of the wall. If this un-American Congress would have an epiphany, which will not happen as long as democrats resist, revile, and refuse to do what they said they would do years ago, our country would save enough money in six-months to pay for the wall in its entirety.

Ten-stop all illegal immigrant fund transfers from the U.S. to Mexico, Honduras, Guatemala, and El Salvador. These appear to be the greatest offenders. Stop Western Union and any other funds transfer agent from performing these wire transactions. Financial incentive needs to be eliminated. We know that tens of billions of dollars are remitted to their countries from the U.S. annually.[26] Why should this nation employ people who remit their discretionary income back to their home country? Citizens of this country clearly spend the preponderance of their income within the U.S. This is one of the things which fuels the economy and keeps America financially fit and strong. If you earn your money in America, spend the preponderance of it here. Most of us are in total agreement with President Trump—America first!

If the 10-steps above were followed, it would not take long to secure our border and ensure our sovereignty and national security. There should be a much needed 11th step, but as long as democrats control Congress, they will never agree to overhaul U.S. broken immigration laws; however, President Trump can initiate action on the ten-steps listed above without enlisting the help of Congress.

The next chapter, Chapter 3, discusses another very important issue to the American people—health care!

———

Endnotes

1   Library of Congress – Progressive Era to New Era, 1900-1929 – Immigrants in Progressive Era – http://www.loc.gov/teachers/classroommaterials/Presentationsandactivities/presentations/ti ...

2   Migration Policy-Naturalization Trends in the United States – https://www.Migrationpolicy.org/article/naturalization-trends-united states/

3   https://immigration-law.freeadvice.com/immigration-law/citizenship/us_filing_len...

4   https://www.newsmax.com/politics/citizenship-clause-constitution-slavery/2018/10/30/id/8...

5   https://en.wikipedia.org/wiki/List_of_United_States_immigration_laws

6   Ibid.

7   Koestler, Fred L. (May 26, 2006) – Operation Wetback 1954 President Eisenhower – *Free Republic* – http://www.freerepublic.com/focus/f-bloggers/1638817/posts

8   History.com Editors – Dwight D. Eisenhower – https://www.history.com/topics/us-presidents/dwight-d-eisenhower

9   History.com Editors – (Updated on February 7, 2019) – U.S. Immigration Since 1965 – https://www.history.com/immigration/us-immigration-since-1965

10 Ibid.

11 https://en.wikipedia.org/wiki/Tip_O'Neil

12 Plumer, Brad (January 30, 2013) *Economic Policy* – Congress tried to fix immigration back in 1986. Why did it fail? – https://www.washingtonpost.com/news/wonk/wp/2013/01/30/in-1986-congress-tried-to-so...

13 https://en.wikipedia.org/wiki/List_of_United_States_immigration_laws

14 Straub, Steve (July 5, 2014) *USNews* – Is The Cloward-Piven Strategy Being Used To Destroy America? – https://thefederalistpapers.org/us/is-the-cloward-Piven-strategy-being-used-to-destroy-ame...

15 Simpson, James (September 28, 2008) *American Thinker* – Barack Obama and the Strategy of Manufactured Crisis – https://

www.americanthinker.com/articles/2008/09/barack_obama_and_the_strategy.html

16 Cuthbertson, Charlotte (January 13, 2019) *THE EPOCH TIMES* – Human Trafficking, Sexual Assaults Key Aspects of Crisis on Southern Border – https://www.theepichtimes.com/human-trafficking-sexual-assaults-key-aspects-of-crisis

17 Ibid., pg. 2

18 Grillo, Ioan / Mexico City (July 31, 2013) The Mexican Drug Cartels' Other Business: Sex Trafficking – TIME.com – http://world.time.com/2013/07/31/the-mexican-drug-cartels-other-business-sex-trafficking/

19 Ibid.

20 Walters, Jim & Davis, Patricia (2011) Human Trafficking, Sex Tourism, and Child Exploitation on the Southern Border, *Journal of Applied Research on Children: Informing Policy for children at Risk*, Vol. 2, Article 6, Published by Digital Commons@The Texas Medical Center, 2011

21 Carr, Grace (may 13, 2019) Drug Abuse is Rampant Across U.S. DC Ranks Worst, –https://thepoliticalinsider.com/drug-abuse-is-rampant-across-us-ranks-worst/?utm_source=conservativedirect&utm_medium=email&utm_campaig...

22 Ibid.

23 Longmire, Sylvia (*Columnist, in Homeland Security*) Recent Drug Seizures Demonstrate Border Wall's Ineffectiveness, https://inhomelandsecurity.com/recent-drug-seizures-demonstrates-border-walls-ineffective...

24 Stevens, Josh (May 29, 2019) I Toured The Texas-Mexico Border. Here are 8 Things I Learned, https://www.leapfrogamerica.com/i-toured-the-texas-mexico-border-here-are-8-things-i-learned/

25 Martinez, Aaron (May 28, 2019) *El Paso Times*, Kris Kobach gives tour of GoFundMe border wall, https://www.elpasotimes.com/story/news/immigration/2019/05/28/border-wall-tour-kris-kobach-gofund...

26 Aizenman, Nurith (February 10, 2017) NPR News, Mexicans In The U.S. Are Sending Home More Money Than Ever, https://www.npr.org/sections/goatsandsoda/2017/02/10/514172676/mexicans-in-the-u-s-are-...

Chapter 3

Health Care Charade

"If you like your doctor, you can keep your doctor, if you like your plan, you can keep your plan," according to President Barack Hussein Obama who stated these bald-faced lies more than two dozen times. Most Americans only wish that those were the only lies he told. He also said that families would receive, on average, $2,500 as a windfall. In fact, what actually happened was the Patient Protection and Affordable Care Act (Affordable Care Act-ACA) resulted in premiums going through the roof, costing most American families $10,000 plus annually with deductible levels of thousands of dollars. By the end of Obama's reign of duplicity, some of us were suffering from prevarication fatigue.

When this irresponsible law was finally ruled on June 28th of 2012 by the Supreme Court, We the People were betrayed again by a 5-4 vote. Most conservatives felt reasonably certain that the Court would strike this nonsensical law down, but justice was not served all because of Chief Justice John Roberts who went rogue with his tortured opinion which upheld the ACA. In an unusual move, three conservative justices joined together in a written minority dissent. In Justice Roberts' defense, it has been suggested that he had been coerced into upholding the law, because of a skeleton in his closet. Should that not be the case, let's extrapolate his thinking. If the federal government can force the American people to purchase a product, and in this case insurance, then why can't the government dictate which automobile I drive, house I purchase, or washing machine and dryer I buy? What about the ruling of the Supreme Court regarding whether or not the Commerce Department could include a question on the 2020 census about citizenship? Roberts, once again, sided with the liberal court in a 5-4 decision on June 27, 2019 to disallow the asking of whether or not a person is a citizen of this country in the course of conducting the census. In this decision, he obviously meddled in the conduct of the federal government's business, because he and others wanted to know *why* this question was apropos relative to its pertinence in the collecting of census data. That is not the purpose of the Supreme Court. His and the other lefty loonies, garbed in black robes, were there to determine constitutionality of an action by the federal government. So much for the lack of professionalism and conservativism by Roberts.

Regardless of what flawed research states, America has the best "health care" in the world; besides, this whole phony charade is about nothing more than socializing America's medical and insurance systems. The aim of the delusional Democrat Party is to enslave the American citizenry with a single-payer system, that is, total federal government control. They want cradle to grave direction of all-American lives. They want socialism, and that is not what the Founders of this great republic created. Other than capitalism, all other forms of government have failed, and socialism has enslaved hundreds of millions of people around the globe. "By the end of the 20th century, socialism had been responsible for the deaths of nearly a half-billion people worldwide, with many hundreds of millions more maimed, traumatized and enslaved."[1] Hopefully, voters have not forgotten that not one Republican in the House voted for this fraudulent law. This unconstitutional piece of trash belongs solely to Obama and the Democrat Party. They own it.

What's really sad is that the Republican Party controlled the House, Senate, and the Presidency 2016-2018, but did little to correct this terrible law. Somehow, they must have had a collective-selective memory loss; however, the passage of the GOP Tax Cuts and Jobs Act finally killed the insane individual mandate of the ACA. President Trump had eagerly waited for a clean bill which completely repealed the ACA, but that bill never arrived on his desk. Even though, many of them, as candidates, promised to rectify this injustice. In the Senate, Senator John McCain, who was dying of brain cancer, left his Arizona home and arrived in the wee hours of the morning at the U.S. Capitol and gave a defiant thumbs down on the bill. Candidly, he should not have been allowed to vote, he was very ill of brain cancer of all things. It had been reported that Senator Mitch McConnell, Majority Leader, had been assured that Senator McCain was going to vote for the repeal and replacement of the ACA, but something happened before the vote which caused him to go in the opposite direction. In a recent discussion with one of my daughters, who was personally knowledgeable of someone close to her who had just passed away because of brain cancer, believed he was not mentally stable enough to even vote. Perhaps, that was the case, but there were two other F-Rs (fake republicans) Susan Collins of Maine and Lisa Murkowski of Alaska who deserted the GOP majority as well.[2] Of course, all the delusional democrats voted against the bill. They are monolithic in their effort to create a socialist America.

If the Republican Party had not squandered two years of its control of the House, this disgusting piece of legislation would have been repealed and replaced in the first 60 days of the 115th Congress, and President Trump would have gladly signed it into law, but that was not to be. The GOP did not even have something with which to replace the ACA. The Speaker of the House, Paul Ryan, despised President Trump and did everything he could to subvert the Trump agenda. He began acting as though he had been elected as the President of the United States. He was elected to serve the citizens of District 1 in Wisconsin, and as Speaker of the House, where weak-kneed bellicose republican colleagues voted for him to serve as Speaker.

Try for a minute or so to imagine yourself as president, working with these devious and duplicitous characters on a daily basis. How awful it must be for President Trump who is an honorable person, a loving father and husband, working like an automaton on a mission to make America great again, while his efforts are subverted at every turn by career politicos, liberal judges, civil servants, political appointees, the Deep State, print and electronic media (especially TV), delusional democrats, and fake republicans (F-Rs). His focus and intensity are beyond amazing, and at times, they even seem to approach the supernatural. In my lifetime, I've never seen a person so verbally battered 24/7 and still multitasks with agility and alacrity, jokes, smiles, and keeps on winning for America. That is a great man, phenomenon, and president. I know of no one who could equal this man's achievements. Yet, his enemies and adversaries portray him as heartless and uncaring, all the while he is doing good for the citizens of America, especially older citizens. What he has done about the cost of prescription drugs is truly special and very meaningful. I cannot recall a former president really focusing in on the pharmaceutical robbery by big Pharma like President Trump.

He has even made phone calls to CEOs of several of the giants in the pharmaceutical industry to request that they find ways to lower the costs and some have done so.

Prescription Drugs

Though the high prices of drugs have little effect on the Trump family, President Trump fully understands with what most Americans have to contend in order to fill a prescription. Sometimes, they have to make choices among other necessities in order to afford a particular drug. Because of this dichotomy, the president has encouraged the purchasing of needed drugs from other countries such as Canada, especially when they can be obtained for half the price or better than U.S. prices. There used to be a saying by a brokerage firm, E.F. Hutton, who used the adage in its commercials in the 1970s and 1980s "When E.F. Hutton speaks, people listen." That's what nearly everyone now says about President Trump. He does not shy away from conflict or inflammatory remarks which he is willing to back up with affirmative action. In October of 2018, he signed two executive orders—the Lowest Prices Act and the Patients' Right to Know Drug Prices Act. The latter executive order promotes greater transparency regarding pharmaceutical pricing.[3] This is noteworthy, but the Congress should write and enact law which embraces these executive orders. Of course, anytime he singles out a particular industry, the stock market, temporarily, reacts negatively. President Trump speaks plainly, bluntly, and without reservation. He has said that pharmaceutical companies are getting away with murder.[4] He also said, "This is a total rip off, and we are ending it."[5] Critics may say what they wish, but Donald J. Trump acts and is willing to take the heat; moreover, he has made it clear that he does not want campaign donations from the pharmaceutical industry. In 2016, his campaign received nearly $387,000 from donors working in the industry; whereas, the democrat nominee, Hillary Clinton, garnered $2.7 billion in donations.[6]

Not all Drugs Are Good

It is without question that we have an opioid epidemic in America with about 70,000 fatal overdoses annually. There are at least two prescription opioid drugs which have been under the microscope for some time— OxyContin and Fentanyl. Both of these drugs have been widely used in pain management and in some cases with disastrous results.

> *America is in the midst of a twenty-year public health crisis that can be traced to 1995, when Richard Sackler started Purdue Pharma and the company introduced OxyContin to the U.S. market. It's estimated that the family has seen double digit billions in revenue from this pill, which was marketed to prescribers and patients as "the pain pill to start with and stay with."*[7]

Though Purdue Pharma denies any wrongdoing, the company has been forced to file bankruptcy as part of a settlement of approximately $12-billion.[8] OxyContin is clearly an addictive drug even though it was marketed differently, and now perhaps Purdue will have to pay litigants.

Then, there is Fentanyl another highly addictive and deadly synthetic drug, which initially seemed to help with the management of pain; however, "Americans are dying of opioid overdoses at an alarming rate. And fentanyl, a drug created in labs in the 1960s, is among the biggest killers."[9] This is a legal drug, but China has been very involved in drug trafficking, especially to the United States. China's labs have been turning out tens of thousands of pounds of this deadly synthetic killer and much of it comes over the U.S. southern border. This is one of the reasons President Trump has been very intense and vigorous in getting a physical barrier between Mexico and the U.S. erected. He disdains these drugs and rails against them.

While President Trump is doing his job for the American people, the leftist delusional democrats do nothing but fire negative salvos at him. They want to impeach, investigate, prosecute, and persecute him rather than serve their districts or states. On May 9, 2019, at the

White House, President Trump urged Congress to write legislation which would protect patients from "surprise" medical bills "from out-of-network doctors that can unnecessarily cost patients tens of thousands of dollars."[10] Clearly, this is an important issue which has always needed attention, but if the democrat controlled House does any work on this or anything positive, it will be completely out of character. Apparently, their purpose is to hate and try to destroy President Trump.

Health Care a Right or Privilege?

Simply stated, it depends on whom you ask. A dozen people will say it's a privilege, and another dozen ardently and vehemently proclaim it to be a right. No where in the Constitution is health care specifically enumerated one way or another, unlike the specificity of the right to bear arms as put forth in the Second Amendment. Even that amendment is foolishly questioned by leftist judges and other ignorant liberals who tend to hate America rather than thank God we live in such one-of-a-kind nation. The Founders of our country were not concerned about hunting game, they were troubled by the possibility of a tyrannical government running roughshod, at some time in the future, over the citizenry; therefore, the citizens should be armed.

I only wish that the minority of American citizens, who embrace socialism, would just go to a socialist country where they can be a part of that health care system. There are two nearby—Cuba and Venezuela. They should stop trying to change our country into something they desire and just move! As a citizen patriot, I will pay the transportation costs of any socialist couple who will leave this country; however, that couple must remain in the country of their choice for at least 10 years and rescind their American citizenship before departure. Rather than wasting your money to keep electing F-Rs (fake republicans), I urge all American patriots to act in kind and make this financial sacrifice so that we can have capitalism, life, liberty, and the pursuit of happiness the American way.

Dr. Howard Bauchner, MD, Editor in Chief, *Journal of the American Medical*

Association (JAMA), believes that health care is a right.[11] Is it possible that he just might be taking a self-interested position? It should be noted that only about a quarter of the physicians within the U.S. are members of the American Medical Association (AMA). I wonder why. Among other things, could it be that 75% of physicians are roiled with the AMA over the health care brouhaha? It seems that the numbers speak for themselves. Perhaps, health care is a right and a privilege. I have a right to own just about anything, but if I don't have the funds with which to purchase something, though I have the right, I can't afford myself of it, even though, it would be a privilege for me to possess it. I have the right to offer to purchase Trump Tower, but it's highly unlikely that President Trump would accept my offer, even though it would be a great privilege to own it. Is it not God who grants us natural rights—such as life and liberty? It is He who allows us to be born and inherit the Earth. It is He who gives us freewill to choose our paths in life. It is not a right to serve God, but it is a great honor and privilege to rejoice in the joys of the Creator.

What does the Constitution state about health care? Only a progressive liberal or a very confused Supreme Court can read something into the Constitution which is not there and rule from the bench what they think the Founders actually addressed rather than what was intended. The confused and possibly conflicted Chief Justice Roberts actually concluded that the ACA was a tax and that Congress had the Constitutional power to impose it on American citizens. However, President Obama and his people tried to sell it first as a *right* for Americans by abusing and misusing the concept of "general welfare" as written in the preamble of the Constitution or the Commerce Clause, Article I, Section 8, as a tax. The federal government was never intended to be all things to all people. Those who need a nanny state have either been born in or come to the wrong country. This is a republic created by tough rugged individualists who had an unquenchable thirst for liberty and freedom. Most of the Founding Fathers had considerable wealth, but they desired freedom and liberty more than their wealth.

President Trump, in some ways, can be likened to the Founders. The majority were wealthy businessmen and entrepreneurs of means. Many of them inherited significant fortunes. George Washington, Benjamin Franklin, Thomas Jefferson, James Madison, and John

Hancock, just to mention a few, were quite well off. In all, there were 55 men who are considered to be a Founding Father. Another thing they possessed was exceptional intellect. Despite the mindless opinions of delusional democrats, ignorant media hosts, and F-Rs (fake republicans) President Donald J. Trump is highly intelligent and perhaps even brilliant. Most students of history consider Thomas Jefferson, James Madison, Benjamin Franklin, and many others, to be brilliant as well. The Founders were determined to initiate a new government, even though it cost them greatly individually and collectively relative to personal wealth. In fact, several of them died penniless. The Founders wanted to devise a great America (AGA), and President Trump has been trying to make America great again (MAGA) so that we can keep America great (KAG). Over the past few decades, America has been stained and tarnished by bad policy and political hijinks. The ACA is a perfect example of this shenanigans. It was shoved down the throats of American citizens. The majority of Americans soundly rejected this socialist attempt to take over the insurance and medical system of the nation; however, since democrats were in control, they ignored the objections of the people, as fascists usually do. Nancy Pelosi led the democrats down the rathole of rottenness with impunity, but the entire republican conference did not comply with her directions, because they *all* voted no for Obamacare (ACA).

The Trump Health Care Executive Order

According to Richard A. Epstein of the Hoover Institution, President Trump's Executive Order of 2017 embraced competition and the opening up of health care markets.

> *President Trump has issued a long overdue Executive Order (EO) opening up health care markets to a new regime of choice and competition. Of course, his liberal detractors are up in arms. . . . There are difficulties, both practical and legal, in undoing the Affordable Care Act (ACA), which should have never been implemented in the first place.*[12]

Epstein went on to elucidate on the efficacy of pricing issues and competition.

The ACA embodies all the pathologies of centrally planned systems by refusing to use prices to signal the relative worth of various goods. Worse, it requites all providers to allocate their expenditures between medical services and administrative expenses under its 80/20 Rule (or 85/15 for large insurers). . . . The EO's first step is to "facilitate the purchase of health insurance across state lines. . . ." No one knows how the new EO will play out. But it marks a major advance over the ACA and has the virtue of not being a bowdlerized version of the Republican's failed repeal-and-replace program. It's too bad the policies contained in the EO were not tried sooner.[13]

It can be reasoned that this fraudulent health care law is akin to a rare cancer inserted into the body politic of the U.S.A. This disease has metastasized, because some misguided Americans now think that Obamacare is a good thing. According to *Kaiser Health News*, 50 percent of those polled supported the ACA, while 46 percent had a negative view of the law.[14] One of the reasons why this might be happening is because once something has become a part of our society, it's difficult to eliminate it. This albatross has been law for nearly a decade (2010) as it has flapped its powerful wings in defiance of individual liberty and freedom in the face of American citizens. The ACA is just one more bowl of stale socialist cereal.

President Trump is in touch with the wants, needs, and desires of the American public, and he still intends to repeal Obamacare in its entirety.[15] He also knows that republicans do not want to pursue that aim now, because as long as the Democrat Party is in charge of the House, nothing will be done. It is truly the *venal do-nothing party*, except resist, revile, and obstruct the Trump administration. This gaggle of socialists would love to see the Constitution burning brightly from a match which they hope to strike. They are such a disgusting lot, always whittling away at liberty and freedom, thinking only of their twisted and sick philosophy; however, the president understands these miscreants and has a logical approach in dealing with them.

According to tweets from the president, "Vote will be taken right after the [2020] Election when Republicans hold the Senate & win . . . back the House."[16] In another tweet, he made it clear that the ACA was a terrible law. He said, "Everybody agrees that ObamaCare doesn't work. Premiums & deductibles are far too high – Really bad HealthCare!"[17]

Dr. Robert Moffit of the Heritage Foundation made some observations regarding the Left's desperation regarding the president's health care plan. Apparently, Steny Hoyer, House Majority Leader, has been coming unglued with all sorts of verbal attacks on the Trump administration in which he has proclaimed that the administration is guilty of "ongoing sabotage" of the ACA. Dr. Moffit concluded that, "As far as "sabotage," Obamacare sabotaged Obamacare."[18] He reasoned that:

> *Over the last four years, Obamacare delivered soaring health insurance premium costs in the exchanges (jumping 105% between 2013 and 2017 alone); many thousands of dollars in individual and family deductible; a collapse of choice and competition in the individual insurance markets; a flattening and declining exchange enrollment; and a progressive reduction in patients' choice of physicians and medical facilities. Today, 72% of Obamacare plans have narrow provider networks.*

This certainly sounds more logical and reasonable than an emotional and delusional democrat like Steny Hoyer who has been around Washington since Moby Dick was a minnow—another poster-child for term limits.

Secrecy and Transparency

As a businessman, President Trump is keenly aware of how to conduct business and shady and questionable practices are unacceptable. The lack of transparency and the secretive nature of health care pricing can be compared to the Truth in Lending Act of 1968 which required all financial institutions to be completely forthright and transparent when dealing with the consumers of America. Consumers of medical services have the same right to be informed about what they must pay for a specific drug, medical procedure, or the services of a medical professional. This is not to suggest that all providers of medical services should charge the same amount. Actually, it is quite the opposite, because of the need to introduce marketplace competitiveness into the health care milieu.

According to Robert Pear of *The New York Times*, "Price transparency has been a hallmark of health policy under Mr. Trump. In a country that spends more than $3.5 trillion a year on health care, administration officials say, it is absurd that consumers cannot shop for medical goods and services as they shop for airline tickets and electronic gear."[19] Pear also cited what administration officials have said about the inexplicable wide range of differences in pricing for specific medical procedures. "In Minnesota, it said, insurers pay as much as $47,000 and as little as $6,200 for a total knee replacement operation. For a total hip replacement, payments have ranged from $6,700 to $44,000."[20]

Behaviorally, looking at what consumers actually do when they try to purchase most things, they usually allow three basic factors to influence their decision—price, value, and quality—but not necessarily in that order. If a person is shopping for a new car or a new pair of shoes, these are preeminent concerns. Why should medical services or procedures be different? Why is it that doctors whom you have never seen or met be allowed to charge a person for professional services about which a patient is unaware? From personal and practical experience, I can speak to this. As a patient, I have had doctors, whom I had never seen or met, charge me for services which they provided during the night as I slept. I didn't request these doctors and was unaware that I was responsible for their services; yet, after my discharge from the hospital, as I perused the bill, I discovered these "ghost physicians" on the hospital bill. What I did by reviewing the charges is somewhat unusual, because it is common for a patient to not care one way or another because of third-person providers—insurance companies. A typical consumer might say something like "The insurance paid for it, I didn't." Anecdotally, I've heard this type of response over the years from many people. A hundred years ago, it was a patient and doctor relationship. You paid the doctor for medical services, not someone else. Now, because of a third-party, most Americans really don't know, factually, the amount paid for medical services. It is without question we need transparency, and that is exactly what the president is trying to achieve, and the Democrat Party staunchly stands in opposition. The election of 2020 is pivotal relative to moving health care forward. The House must flip back to the GOP because of the election of true conservative republicans. The democrats want the status quo. They could care less about what American citizens, think, want, or need. They are motivated and propelled by the need to have power which will put them in charge of the lives of all Americans.

The president is very optimistic about what the republicans will roll out in 2020 regarding a good health care plan. In fact, he has gone so far as to make the comment that the Republican Party would soon be known as the "party of health care." Joel Pollack of Breitbart has enumerated what he considers to be health care achievements of President Trump. According to Pollack, he sees 10 specific accomplishments of the President, which include: lower premiums, short-term plans, *end to the individual mandate*, group health plans across state lines, choice for veterans, right to try, drug price information, made opioids and fentanyl a priority, better administration, and support for repeal.[21] Of the ten items listed, the ending of the individual mandate has had a widespread impact on American citizens. This, essentially was the soul of Obamacare. Before extracting this poison from the law, American citizens were having to pay significant fines for *not* purchasing insurance through Obamacare—reminiscent of pre-world II fascist Nazi Germany where the state took precedent over the individual. The democrats led by Barack Hussein Obama and his minions did that *to* America. Obamacare is essentially a stake of death driven deeply into the heart of this republic by anti-Americans who despise the Constitution and the brilliant men who created this nation under God.

We the People should never forget that 100% of democrats in the House, along with a handful of F-Rs (fake republicans), are responsible for this deadly anti-America legislative piece of garbage.

These so-called representatives have had an obvious personal agenda, that is, destroy the America of history and drag it down into the depths of depravity and self-interest. The Senate is no better. Just look at the games played in 2017 when a complete repeal of this evil was within reach. Of course, the democrats did what we expected them to do—hold on to this deadly law at all costs, but a handful of deceitful republicans made sure that this unconstitutional law remained in place. What despicable reprobates!

Finally, let's not forget that this law is not really about health care, it is about government control of the lives of American citizens through the use of health care *insurance*. This law does not improve true "health care" one whit. It does not ameliorate the skills and abilities of medical professionals in any way. It only gives government the final say in medical matters. In 2020, we should all only vote for conservative republicans if we really want to repeal the ACA; moreover, that should be a litmus test for anyone for whom we should cast a vote. If a citizen is republican or an independent, the choice is clear, the vote must be cast for the republican, and we can only hope and pray they are not F-Rs. Even if a candidate is a neighbor and friend, it is not advisable to vote for that person if that individual is a democrat or an F-R. Democrats are, for the most part, political terrorists, and F-Rs are reminiscent of surreptitious vipers who are dangerous and may strike at any time; therefore, they should be avoided. We have another opportunity in 2020 to vote for President Trump, and hopefully, conservative republicans, if we are serious about the repeal and replacement of Obamacare. We will finally drive a stake into the heart of this bloodsucking Dracula.

Though health care remains as one of the top issues and concerns of American citizens, Chapter 4, which follows, addresses another critical and highly significant topic, that is, the fervent Trump dynamic economy which is the powerful engine driving our prosperous society.

———

Endnotes

1   Rush, Eric (08/01/2018) Socialism: A Turd By Any Other Name, *WND*, https://www.wnd.com/2018/08/socialism-a-turd-by-any-other-name/Caldwell, Leigh Ann (7/28/2017) *NBC News*, https://www.nbcnews.com/politics/congress/senate-gop-effort-repeal-obamacare-fails-n78...

2   Caldwell, Leigh Ann (7/28/2017) NBC News, https://www.nbcnews.com/politics/congress/senate-gop-effort-repeal-obamacare-fails-n78...

3   Cohen, Joshua (May 27, 2019) Trump Ready To Force Transparency in Healthcare Pricing With An Executive Order, https://www.forbes.com/joshuacohen/2019/05/27/trump-ready-to-force-transparency-...

4   Humer, Caroline & Campos, Rodrigo, Politics (January 11, 2017) *Reuters* https://www.reuters.com/article/us-usa-trump-drugpricing-idUSKBN14V24J

5   CBS / AP (May 11, 2018) Trump announces plan to lower drug prices: "This is a total rip off, and we are ending it" – https://www.cbsnews.com/news/trump-prescription-drug-prices-plan-announcement-2018-...

6   Sink, Justin & Allison, Bill (April 24, 2019) Trump Says He Doesn't Want Campaign Donations From Pharma, https://www.bloomberg.com/news/articles/2019-04-24/trump-opioid-pharmaceutical-donors

7   Goldberg, Sana [RN] (2019) *How To Be A Patient: The essential Guide to Navigating the World of Modern Medicine*, Thorndike Press, pgs. 264-265.

8   Mulvihill, Geoff (September 16, 2019) Purdue Pharma files for bankruptcy as part of settlement, [Associated Press] https//:news.yahoo.com/purdue-pharma-files-bankruptcy-part-032702567.html

9   NPR [Health] (September 1, 2019) A History of Fentanyl, https://www.npr.org/ 2019/09/01/756427945/a-history-of-fentanyl

10 *By Reuters* (May 9, 2019) Trump calls on Congress to protect patients from surprise medical bills, https://www.nbcnews.com/health/health-care/latest-trump-proposes-end-surprise-medical-...

11 Bauchner, Howard-Editorial (January 3, 2017) Health Care in the United States: A Right or a Privilege-https://jamanetwork.com/journals/jama/fullarticle/2595503

12 Epstein, Richard A. (October 16, 2017) Making Health Care Great Again, Hoover Institution, https://www.hoover.org/research/making-health-care-great-again

13 Ibid.

14 Rovner, Julie (December 13, 2017) Why Do People Hate Obamacare, Anyway? *Kaiser Health News*, https://khn.org/news/why-do-people-hate-obamacare-anyway/

15 Brownstein, Ronald (March 21, 2019) President Trump Still Wants to Repeal Obamacare, Politics, *The Atlantic*, https://www.theatlantic.com/politics/archive/2019/03/trumps-health-care-plan-will-influe...

16 Kiggins, Steve (April 2, 2019) In a series of late-night tweets, Trump says Republicans' health care plan will go to vote after 2020 election, *USA Today*, https://www.usatoday.com/story/news/politics/2019/04/01//trump-republicans-health-plan-vote-after-202...

17 Ibid.

18 Moffit, Robert (April 3, 2019) Why the Left Is Desperate to Sabotage Trump's Health Care Plans, [Health Care Commentary] Daily Signal.com, https://www.dailysignal.com/2019/04/03/why-the-left-is-desperate-to-sabotage-trumps-hea...

19 Pear, Robert (March 8, 2019) Trump Administration Targets 'Secretive Nature' of Health Care Pricing, *The New York Times*, http://www.nytimes.com/2019/03/08/us/politics/trump-health-care-rates.html

20 Ibid.

21 Pollack, Joel (March 28, 2019) Pollack: President Trump's Top 10 Health Care Achievements, Breitbart, https://www.breitbart.com/health/2019/03/28/   President-trump-achievements-on-health-car...

Chapter 4

The Trump Dynamic Economy

While moronic and ignorant people run around blathering nonsensical statements in front of TV cameras about President Trump not being responsible for this roaring economy, critical measures of success such as, employment levels, Job creation, inflation level, wage increases, gross domestic product (GDP), energy prices are all positive, and the Trump administration made it all happen in less than three years, and that is without the assistance of the media, radical democrats, and fake republicans (F-Rs). Can anyone imagine how well he could have done with genuine support? Forget about support, how about not resisting the president's every move. Though not necessarily a good economic indicator, but even the stock market is at historic highs. Obama and Biden had absolutely nothing to do with it. They and the rest of their democrat colleagues severely damaged America in eight years of economic retrenchment, fecklessness, decay, and malaise.

According to Monica Crowley, we now have a robust economy which has leftists "petrified". "Last week brought economic news so good that it sent the democrats and their fellow travelers in the Resistance Media into full bury-then-ignore mode."[1] Leftists are not interested in factual information. They live in a delusional and fictional world where thinking men and women dare not trod. Democrats are not interested in common sense or logic. Their engines are fueled by emotion, accusation, and prevarication. They usually out-of-hand reject factual information, because that gets in the way of political expediency. Crowley also stated, "Unemployment rates among blacks, Latinos and women are at or near historic lows."[2] A quick review of Labor Force Statistics from the Current Population substantiates her claim.[3]

Unemployment Rate Facts

In reviewing the U.S. unemployment rate by year, it's interesting to note that at about the same time in their terms President Obama and President Trump experienced significantly differing results. Obama was at a rate of 9.10% on January 1, 2011, and Trump saw a much lower unemployment rate at 4.10% on January 1, 2018.[4] These particular numbers in and of themselves don't really show the larger picture, because a closer examination of the numbers clearly demonstrate that Obama and his administration consistently experienced higher levels of unemployment rates than President Trump and his people, thus far. The month of May 2019 unemployment rate of 3.6% is challenging the 3.40% rate of 1969.[5] This is a notable achievement because the record is within reach.

Job Creation

President Trump has excelled in job creation. Through his personal efforts, he is responsible for thousands upon thousands of jobs returning to America. Before this great accomplishment, President Obama had made ignorant and perhaps even stupid remarks about "how" President Trump was going to bring back jobs. He even suggested that perhaps the president would have to use a "magic wand" for this purpose; how puerile. The president understood full-well how to revive the U.S. job market, and he has been doing it constantly over the past three years. Obama was always at a disadvantage, because he knew nothing about real work and job creation. President Trump is a true capitalist who ran a complex international business; whereas, Obama never had a real job or created one. Additionally, in his formative years, he was influenced greatly by a cadre of undesirables such as his own father and Frank Marshal Davis—a devout communist, and later by two anarchists and domestic terrorists by the names of Bill Ayers and Bernadine Dohrn.

Obama had given up on America regarding manufacturing jobs. He even suggested that this would be the "new normal," just as he said about a GDP of about 1.5%. Trump has turned this infantile thinking completely around by being responsible for adding more than 400,000 manufacturing jobs to the economy in less than three years. Immediately after taking office in January of 2017, he authorized the use of several energy pipelines which brought about the addition of tens of thousands of jobs, as well as the opening up of the oil fields of Anwar in Alaska. Just think, we are now energy independent for the first time in about 75 years!

Because of Trump's business savvy and strategy, auto makers are finding their way back to America, and they are bringing bucket loads of money for the purpose of refurbishing or building new automobile facilities. Reuters reported, "U.S. President Donald Trump on Saturday said at a rally that Japanese Prime Minister Shinzo Abe told him Japan is investing $40 billion in new car factories in the United States."[6] This is proof that a lot of business is often transacted on the golf course. After all, President Trump and Prime Minister Abe did play a round at of one of President Trump's golf courses.

In President Trump's first two years he blew away Obama's meager efforts regarding job creation. "There's no contest. President Trump's first two years, blew away Barack Obama's in the field of jobs. . . . Forbes reported that 312,000 jobs were added in December and that manufacturing is growing 714 percent faster under President Trump than Obama."[7] As of April of 2019, job creation was punctuated by the addition of 263,000 new jobs which outstripped the projection of 213,000 by a significant margin.[8] It's almost humorous watching and listening to economic gurus who keep trying to predict what the Trump administration is able to accomplish. At times, it almost seems as though some of them are disappointed that President Trump keeps charging along with reckless abandon with a smile on his face while leaving democrats, F-Rs, the leftist media, and other Trump haters stupefied, frustrated, and furious that he really gets things done with, ironically, bombastic aplomb. My guess is when he announced on June 18, 2019, in Orlando, Florida, during his formal kick off of the 2020 campaign, that since he was elected, 6,000,000 new jobs have been added to the U.S. economy, liberal heads exploded around the country. Since Luke AFB is nearby where we live, at first, I thought it was F-35s making those sounds, and it was. We watched them with glee as they flew in formation. To make matters worse for these anti-Americans, this all happened within two-and-a-half years of his presidency.

Inflation Level

All Americans should be thankful that we no longer experience incredibly high inflation or the high interest rates of democrat President Jimmy Carter, Jr. 1977-1981. When he came into office, the inflation rate was 5.22% and ended up at 11.83% upon his departure.[9] Interest rates actually reached a high of 18%. Over the years, the inflation rate has remained relatively low, that is, typically 2-3%. As of May 2019, the rate was 1.8%.[10] The reason that inflation rates are important is they are good indicators of a strong or weak economy. Generally, lower inflation rates and/or interest rates are desirable for a strong economy. The stock markets do especially well in a strong economy. Since President Trump was elected, the financial markets have added approximately $10 trillion of wealth. That is a very impressive number. When the market soars, it generally shows that investors have confidence in the overall health of the economy. At this point in the Trump presidency, it appears the financial markets are quite pleased and so is every American who relies upon the financial strength of the U.S. economy, which includes those with 401ks as well as retirees.

Wage Growth

It has been reported frequently in the media that middle class American worker wages have been flat for nearly two decades, as the middle class shrunk. Neither the Bush or Obama administrations moved the needle on this problem. President Trump and his administration have done a remarkable job. Over the past three years, that situation has changed dramatically. Wages have finally begun to rise nationally by as much as 3%. The return of jobs from abroad, increased manufacturing productivity, new and increased energy production and sources have finally resulted in marginal wage increases. It appears that this, historically, intractable issue will continue to move in a positive direction as long as a capitalist such as President Trump is leading America. Democrat socialism will not get it. Socialists have little to no actual comprehension of how and why capitalism works. Without trying to sound trite, it's as though they believe that there is a large standing of money trees which dot the countryside, and when funds are needed, just harvest the money leaves. This analogy probably sounds ridiculous, but so is socialism.

Gross Domestic Product (GDP)

In order to appreciate how far the U.S. has come under the leadership of President Trump relative to the GDP, we must look back to where the U.S. GDP was under the leadership of President Obama. Succinctly stated, the Obama record was abysmal. During the eight years of his presidency, the U.S. *never* reached a 3% growth level. He was the one who stated that the new normal for GDP in America would hover around the 1% growth rate going forward. He had no idea that President Trump could cause things to happen in such extraordinary ways. "Not only is the average annual growth rate of just 1.48% during Obama's business cycle the weakest of any expansion since at least 1949, he has just become the only President to have not had even one year of 3% GDP growth."[11] President Trump reached and surpassed the 3% GDP growth rate in two-and-a-half years. "The GDP rate is at 3%-something the Obama administration thought impossible."[12] Trump is a professional and Obama, at best, is/was an amateur.

Energy Independence

Many of us patriots, and some of us for decades, have always believed that the United States of America could and should have been energy independent long, long ago. Primarily, it did not happen until now because of greedy globalist leaders—especially presidents—environmental wackos, delusional democrats, maladroit media, and just plain old rotten to the core corrupt politicians, of which, this country certainly has more than its share. Politically, we are not much better than third-world dictatorships. Just look what Crooked Hillary and her minions tried to do to overthrow the presidency of President Trump. They created a witch hunt that dogged the Trump administration for nearly three years. Our representatives, in general, of our representative republic, are bought and sold on a daily basis by lobbyists and other immoral, unethical, and soulless minions who hate America.

What has changed? What has caused America to breathe the sweet air of freedom, liberty, and true capitalism once again? Simple, it took a billionaire who did not need money to allow America to be America again. It took a person who had wealth and means to walk through the dark door of putrid decomposition of the body politic. He needed none of these pathetic amoral hacks. He needed none of their foul-smelling money. He needed We the People, and Donald J. Trump snatched the mantle of leadership from one of the most corrupt, rotten, and evil human beings to ever walk this Earth. I, for one, pray for President Trump and his family each and every day, while I thank God for giving us a true leader.

Immediately upon his assumption of the presidency, President Trump began flinging open the energy floodgates. He quickly signed executive orders which allowed the XL and Dakota pipelines to move forward full speed which included pipelines for natural gas, and of course, environmentalists, liberals, and certain American Indians, howled louder than a pack of coyotes, but the Trump administration prevailed.[13] He has granted the opening up of the Anwar oilfield in Alaska. He encouraged oil drilling, coal mining, shale production, and fracking everywhere in the U.S. where it made sense. The U.S. is now producing more than 12,000 barrels of oil per day. Additionally, the U.S. has a wealth of natural gas. Based on current usage, it is estimated that the U.S. has about another 80-90 years of natural gas.

For the first time in decades, coal mines began to reopen, and to this day, the media refuses to give credit to President Trump for shining the spotlight of truth on the viability and need for clean coal.[14] What president in the past 30 years has emphasized the importance of coal as compared to Trump? The answer is none. There is no comparison, but that does not stop the dishonest and disgraceful media from obfuscating and denying that both Trump and coal are awesome.

It is undeniable that President Trump has taken Herculean action in rolling back job-killing regulations which were mostly imposed by Obama in his quest to destroy the coal industry among other sources of energy. Obama's words still ring in the ears of patriotic Americans when he proclaimed that electricity was going to "necessarily skyrocket" primarily because of the costs of coal. According to him, the regulations he set in place would make it virtually impossible for coal to continue to be one of the USA's energy sources. Obama was and still is a disgraceful and despicable human being who, to this day, continues to do all he can to damage and injure President Trump and the USA.

Real Regulatory Relief

It is has been well-established over time that red tape, rules, and regulations have been strangling America for decades. When President Trump took office, he made it clear that the regulatory burden would be reduced. He issued Executive Order 13771 . . . [which] "requires that 'for every new regulation issued, at least two prior regulations be identified for elimination, and that the cost of planned regulations be prudently managed and controlled through a budgeting process.'"[15] The president vowed that for every new regulation implemented, two would be cancelled. According to Clyde Wayne Crews of *FORBES*, by the spring of 2019, the ratio was 2.2 to 1 with the caveat that "it's getting tougher."[16] Apparently, early on, it was easier to accomplish this ratio because of obvious regulations which needed to be eliminated.

> *For its part, the administration should pursue regulatory transparency and accountability reform to help economic growth continue. Even if President Trump were to become distracted by higher-profile issues, his early regulatory reforms have contributed to the nation's current healthy economic growth. He should expand on that success and encourage*

> *Congress to join in – after all, they're incumbents,*
> *too.*[17]

It has been abundantly clear for decades that the energy sector of the U.S. economy has been hamstrung by the federal government because of onerous rules, regulations, and policies which have stood in recalcitrant defiance of progress. Other countries throughout the world, such as India, China, and Russia, have not had to contend with this economic blockade. They have had free reign to do whatever needed to be done to bolster the economies of their countries. This is not to suggest that the U.S. become as reckless and careless as other nations, but it is important to reduce and eliminate unnecessary regulations which restrain economic growth. For the U.S. economy to grow, the U.S. must not be at a disadvantage in a competitive world.

Trump Tariffs

Tariffs are somewhat unusual for America. Practically all of our trading partners levy significant tariffs on our goods, but we have not been placing tariffs on goods coming from other nations. That is one of the reasons we have been running huge deficits with China. China has always levied significant tariffs on our products, but historically, we have not done that to them. Since China joined the World Trade Organization in 2001, the U.S. has been the loser. Essentially, America has rebuilt China over the past decade. To some, that might not mean much, but it has cost the U.S. about $5 trillion in real wealth. First, China does not play by anyone's rules. Second, they do what they consider to be in China's best interest, and third, they have been stealing U.S. intellectual property with reckless abandon on top of massive trade deficits for many years. For example, the U.S. trade deficit with China was $419 billion in 2018, and these types of deficits go back many years.

The president has begun to use the tariff as an economic and *political* tool. He was finally able to cause the Mexican government to move off dead center and do something about the invading hordes from the South American countries of El Salvador, Honduras, and

Guatemala who crashed over the southern border of Mexico and was transported to their northern border—the U.S.-Mexico border. At first, President Trump had a rocky start with the left-leaning President Andres Manuel Lopez Obrador, but after President Obrador sent 6,000 national guard and regular troops to Mexico's southern border, the tide of illegal aliens was stemmed to some degree. Then, President Obrador sent another nearly 15,000 troops to its northern border with the U.S., and that has cut the number of migrant invaders down significantly.[19]

When the Trump administration first began levying tariffs on China, the Establishment sycophants went ballistic, yelling that the sky was falling and the economy would tank because of this ill-conceived notion. Economists, business professionals, politicos, along with the left-wing media, were all beside themselves. They, for the most part, had conniption fits with gnashing of teeth; however, the 10% tariff, after the U.S. stock market got its act together, was taken in stride by the Chinese communist government. Of course, President Trump is also prepared to see that a 25% levy on about another $300 billion of imports come into play in the not too distant future. At the time of this writing, President Trump hopes that he and Xi Jinping will be able to repair their shaky relationship at the upcoming G20 Summit. "President Trump has taken the leverage of economics to levels of geopolitical strategy never seen before. Nowhere is the genius strategy more clear than in the way Trump has positioned the trade reset and confrontation with China."[20] Later, a more in-depth discussion on trade will be pursued.

In summary, the U.S. economy can be likened to a roaring fire fueled by powerful winds of great leadership. President Trump stays out front and takes the heat because he sits high in the saddle where he can easily be seen by his detractors. He backs down from no one; yet, he is always willing to negotiate—unlike the delusional Democrat Party which operates from emotion rather than logic and sound reasoning. From now until January of 2025, the U.S. will continue to experience record breaking economic achievements. It is truly unfortunate and sad that our nation is consumed with political maneuvering and posturing, because if the delusional democrats, F-Rs, and left-wing media would support the president and his administration, what we as a nation could accomplish would be astounding.

Though our prolific economic juggernaut remains in the forefront of the minds of American citizens, the effects of international trade relations have a direct relationship to U.S. job growth, gross domestic product, and the overall economic success of the USA. Chapter 5 provides insight into this conundrum.

———

Endnotes

1   Crowley, Monica (January 9, 2019) How the Trump economic miracle shatters the left, *Washington Times*, https://www.washingtontimes.com/news/2019/jan/9/how-the-trump-economic-miracle-sha...

2   Ibid.

3   Labor Force Statistics from the Current Population, https://www.bls.gov/web/Empsit/cpsee_e16.htm

4   National Employment Monthly Update, National Unemployment Rate at 3.6% Through May 2019, https://www.ncsl.org/research/labor-and-employment/National-employment-monthly-update...

5   US Employment Rate by Year, https://www.multpl.com/employment/table/by-year

6   (Reuters) 4-27-2019-Trump: Japan will invest $40 billion in U.S. car factories, https://www.reuters.com/article/us-usa-trump-japan-idUSKCN1S400F

7   MAGA Voter (January 6, 2019) First 2 Years of Trump vs Obama in Job Creation a BLOWOUT! https://magavoter.com/first-2-years-of-trump-vs-obama-in-job-creation-a-blowout/

8   Bartash, Jeffry (May 3, 2019) U.S. creates 263,000 jobs in April as unemployment falls to 49-year low, Market Watch, https://www.marketwatch.com/story/us-creates-263000-jobs-in-april-and-unemployment-f...

9   What was the inflation rate under Jimmy Carter? https://www.answers.com/Q/What_was_the_inflation_rate_under_Jimmy_Carter

10 Current US Inflation Rates: 2009-2019, https://www.usinflationcalculator.com/inflation/current-inflation-rates/

11 Durden, Tyler (January 27, 2017) Barack Obama Is Now The Only President In History To Never Have A Year Of 3% GDP Growth, https://www.zerohedge.com/news/2017-01-27/barack-obama-now-only-president-history-...

12 Hoft, Jim (May 2, 2019) TRUMP ECONOMIC MIRACLE: $9.1 Trillion in New Market Value – Lowest Unemployment Rate of Any

President, 3% GDP, Wages Uphttps://www.thegatewaypundit. com/2019/05/trump-economic-miracle-9-1-trillion-in-new-…

13 Jones, A., Diamond, J., & Krieg, G. (CNN), (January 24, 2017) Trump advances controversial oil pipelines with executive action, https://www.cnn.com/2017/01/24/ politics/trump-keystone-xl-dakota-access-pipelines-exec…

14 Grandoni, Dino (PowerPost) The Energy 202: Coal production is actually up under Trump. Should he get credit? https://www.washingtonpost.com/powerpost/paloma/ the-energy-202/2017/10/12/the-…

15 Gayer, T., Litan, R. & Wallach, P. (October 27, 2017) Evaluating the Trump administration's regulatory reform program, BROOKINGS, https://www.brookings.edu/research/ evaluating-the-trump-administration-regulatory-refor…

16 Crews, Clyde Wayne (May 30, 2019) Trump's Regulatory Reform Agenda by the Numbers (Summer 2019 Update), *FORBES*, https://cei.org/content/trumps-regulatory-reform-agenda-numbers-summer-2019-update

17 Crews, W., & Young, R. (May 7, 2019) President Trump Should Rediscover Regulatory Reform, [Economy & Business], https://www.nationalreview.com/2019/o5/president-trump-should-rediscover-regulatory-re…

18 Bartash, Jeffrey (June 25, 2019) Why the U.S.-China trade deficit is so huge: Here's all the stuff America imports [Economy & Politics] *MarketWatch*, https://www.Marketwatch.com/story/ heres-all-the-stuff-the-us-imports-from-china-that's-ca…

19 Fredericks, Bob (June 24, 2019) Mexico sends 15k troops to US border to stop Migrants, *NEWS*, https://nypost. com/2019/06/24/mexico-sends-15k-troops-to-Us-border-to-stop-migrants/

20 Sundance (June 15, 2019) President Trump Outwits Chairman Xi Jinping Ahead of G-20 Summit, https://theconservativetreehouse. com/2019/06/15/president-Trump-outwits-chairman-xi-jin…

Chapter 5

International Trade Relations

From the beginning, President Trump has made it clear lopsided trade deficits are no longer going to be allowed. Though countless "economists" and other Establishment critics have been crying wolf, that has not stopped the president from insisting that our trading partners around the world understand that America will come first in matters of trade. He has ebulliently stated countless times that America will no longer be the "piggy bank" of the world. As he often says with great zeal and certainty, "Those days are over!"

The president knows how and why he was elected by We the People. Citizens of this nation needed and wanted a change agent who would sweep into Washington as a disruptor, an antiestablishment man of action, who would return America to its former greatness. Though his critics have been legion, he continues to grind onward. According to the hysterical Peter Coy of Bloomberg Businessweek, "Trump's Damage to International Trade Will Take Years to Repair." He also wrote that, "In a matter of days the president has instigated a trade war, insulted the leaders of numerous allies, thrown NATO into shock, labeled the European Union a foe," among many other egregious errors in judgment.[1] Others are just as critical and whiny as Coy. These people refuse to give President Trump any credit for anything. It appears that most of President Trump's detractors think that he is ignorant, unlearned, and not very bright. My-oh-my, how wrong they are!

NAFTA

Let's look at facts. What president in the past 50 years has really done something meaningful and significant about trade which has put America first? With the exception of President Donald J. Trump, the answer is simple—none! Just look at what has been done *to* America. How about the North American Free Trade Agreement

(NAFTA)? That has been an unmitigated disaster for American workers, families, and the wealth of the USA thanks to the democrat President William (Bill) Jefferson Blythe III Clinton. He signed this job killing rancid piece of legislation into law on December 17, 1992.[2] Since he was and is an Establishment-Globalist cabana boy, he and Hillary must have danced into the night, unless he had a pressing planned rendezvous and interlude with Monica or some other available female. It should be noted that President George H.W. Bush, Establishment-fake republican (F-R), fast-tracked this legislation so that his friend, Bill Clinton, could sign NAFTA into law when he became president. Perhaps, there is honor, not necessarily among thieves, but between thieves.

USMCA (US-Mexico-Canada-Agreement)

During his campaign, Donald Trump castigated NAFTA, because he knew it had been a terrible trade agreement for America. Even Ross Perot during his 1992 third-party bid for the presidency told us that NAFTA would be disastrous, that there would be "a giant sucking sound", but his warnings were totally ignored. Trump had watched what it had done *to* America and was eager to rectify the situation as soon as he was elected president. It gave him a great sense of accomplishment to withdraw America from this globalist agreement and to replace it with something not as financially mordacious and malignant as NAFTA. Thus, the USMCA was created to ameliorate the imbalanced, disproportional, and spurious effects of this disdainful agreement. The Trump administration from the beginning supported a quality trilateral trade pact, but things needed to be more on equal footing for each nation.

The concern now is with ratification of the USMCA. The delusional and radical democrats are not about to give President Trump a win; therefore, more political posturing and unhinged cries from the House must be encountered before the Trump administration can declare a victory. Unfortunately, Nancy Pelosi, Speaker of the House, has a very vocal and radical minority of the democrat House who she must placate; moreover, since the good of the American people is of tertiary concern, at best, to the Democrat Party, it may take a protracted period of time to bring about ratification. Mexico has already ratified the USMCA, and Canada wants to time its acceptance with that of the United States, and Apparently, Prime Minister Trudeau of Canada is prepared to execute the document as soon as the USA is ready.[7]

Important changes which the USMCA has incorporated are higher pay for auto workers, more auto parts from member nations, seventy percent of the steel and aluminum used in vehicles must come from Mexico, the U.S. or Canada, dairy restrictions are loosened by Canada, and intellectual property rules have been stiffened. The USMCA takes effect in 2020 and will be renewed every six years with the caveat that it could expire in 2036. It could even be extended until 2052.[8] What this new trade agreement does is to create a better trade environment which should slow the job drain on America and encourage more investment in the U.S., especially relative to the automobile industry. Ultimately, it improves on the financial drain of America while bringing a greater degree of fairness to the world of trade.

Trans-Pacific Partnership (TPP)

As was his idiosyncrasy to undermine America's place in the world, in February of 2015, Barack Obama gave Congress a fast-track to negotiate the terms of the Trans-Pacific Partnership (TPP) which was comprised of 12 countries including the U.S. All countries signed the agreement.[3] This was just one more nail in the coffin of the sovereignty and financial solvency of America and, at the time, candidate Donald Trump knew it. He instinctively saw this new "deal" for what it was. He knew it would continue to deplete the resources of the U.S., and Obama, the Establishment, and Globalists everywhere were joyous about the prospects. The anti-America radical Democrat Party members, F-Rs (fake republicans), Wallstreet, Chamber of Commerce, and others were eager for the Pacific Rim TPP to take hold. Interestingly, Hillary Clinton who was running for the presidency during 2016 tried to verbally distance herself from this new trade deal. She did not say that she had "hoped" the TPP would be the gold standard of trade, rather, she said it would "be" the gold standard for trade. As expected, this ethically derelict and morally bankrupt cretin did not want Donald Trump to use the TPP as a wedge issue in the runup to the election of 2016. Despite her efforts to deflect, Trump grabbed hold of the issue and championed it. In rally after rally, he railed against this awful agreement and the crowds loved it.

After the greediness of the world is stripped away, what really was the TPP? In other words, what were the guts of this deleterious agreement? "The Trans-Pacific Partnership (TPP) was a secretive, multinational trade agreement that threatened to extend restrictive intellectual property (IP) laws across the globe and rewrite international rules on its enforcement. The agreement in its original form fell apart when the United States abandoned it in November 2016 following the U.S. Presidential election."[4] It was clear that newly elected President Donald J. Trump would never sign anything that did not put America first, and this agreement did anything but that. This was just another one of President Trump's kept promises.

The greatest offender of trade deficit with the U.S. is China. The U.S. trade envoy Robert Lighthizer and team had made great progress regarding a fair agreement between the U.S. and China. They were nearing a negotiated deal, when suddenly, in May of 2019, the Chinese delegation rejected all the work the two groups had accomplished up to that point. Everything went back to square one. This was a setback that the U.S. team had not anticipated. They were quite disappointed and somewhat baffled by this reversal of direction. That being said, that did not stop President Trump from reviving talks with China by offering a tariff truce and break for the thieving Chinese company Huawei. "After a high-stakes meeting with Chinese President Xi Jinping, Trump told reporters on Saturday that he also would delay restrictions against Huawei Technologies, Co., letting U.S. companies resume sales to China's largest telecommunications equipment maker."[5] Time will tell if this decision by Trump was a good one. To some, it is a questionable call regarding Huawei, because that company is a band of thieves. The president intends to retain the 10% tariff on China and has put a hold on the increase of 25% on $300 billion of trade. President Trump is in the negotiation process and only he can judge his strategy. It will not take long for the Chinese to show their hand. The U.S. will have to wait, but the president has expressed optimism regarding President Xi Jinping's intentions.

Trading Partner Challenges

Many do not seem to understand that President Trump is a man of practicality and common sense. In his mind, trade should not only be free and fair but reciprocal, that is, if one country charges America tariffs, then the U.S. should charge the exporting country a reciprocal, and at least, an equal tariff. In the president's world, and in the world of reason, trade tariffs should not exist. Tariffs in and of themselves are primarily a barrier to trade. The question comes to mind—why should trade be discouraged? In a perfect world there should be no reason to discourage trade; however, we do not live in such a world, because of greed, avarice, and self-interest, countries tend to lose sight of comparative advantage or even absolute advantage. Both of these theoretical constructs and practices are a part of the world relative to trade. When other nations attempt to exploit the U.S., President Trump objects not just in words but in actions. This man fights back. He is aware of the way the U.S. has been abused over decades, and on his watch, this type of activity must stop. In one of his 2018 tweets President Trump exclaimed, "The United States is insisting that all countries that have placed artificial Trade Barriers and Tariffs on goods going into their country, remove those Barriers & Tariffs or be met with more than Reciprocity by the U.S.A. Trade must be fair and no longer a one way street!"[6]

President Trump is incredibly transparent, and he pulls no punches. Trading partners around the world must accept that this isn't the trade-world of yesteryear. Since the election of President Trump in 2016, there is no more status quo. It is now America first and fairness is a must. He knows why the American people elected him, and he fully intends to keep the promises he made during his campaign. President Trump values loyalty in a great way, and he knows that citizens have been very loyal to him and that really matters.

While the critics continue to shout fire in the movie theater, there are others, such as Peter Navarro, who have a far more optimistic view of the president's trade strategy and policy. "The U.S. trade deficit for goods hit a record high in 2018, but critics wrongly blame this on a failure of President Trump's trade policies. . . . The president's tough trade agenda has also helped bring recalcitrant trading partners to the negotiating table."[9] Navarro went on to say that Congress should act with haste regarding the ratification of the USMCA, because the agreement will boost manufacturing in the U.S. and likely help shrink the trade deficit with Mexico. This is good advice to the Congress, but democrats do not rely on intellectual acuity and rational thinking when it comes to decision making. Their decisions are usually founded in a pot of an emotional quagmire of socialist soup.

In summary, though President Trump's trade strategy and policies are very controversial, it all seems to be working. The tariffs imposed on countries have not resulted in economic devastation as naysayers proclaimed, rather it has been an overall net positive, and the U.S. has received $billions from imposed tariffs. Thankfully, for the most part, America's farmers have been supportive of the president, and he has done what he can to support them. The truth is that American consumers may take a short term hit in the purchasing of products and services, but long-term results, as a nation, will be realized in the not too distant future. International trade and international relations are inextricably intertwined, which is discussed in Chapter 6.

———

Endnotes

1   Coy, Peter (July 19, 2018) Bloomberg Businessweek, Trump's Damage to International Trade Will Take Years to Repair, https://www.bloomberg.com/News/articles/2018-07-19/trump-s-damage-to-international-trade-will-take-years-to-repair

2   Bill Clinton Signs the North American Free Trade Agreement (December 8. 1993) https://worldhistoryproject.org/1993/12/8/bill-clinton-signs-the-north-american-free-trade-...

3   Kenton, Will (Reviewed by-May 7, 2019) Trans-Pacific Partnership (TPP), *Investopedia*, https://www.investopedia.com/terms/t/transpacific-partnership-tpp.asp

4   Electronic Frontier Foundation, Trans-Pacific Partnership Agreement, https://www.eff.org/issues/tpp

5   Donnan, Shawn & Han, Miao (June 29, 2019) Trump Revives China Talks With Tariffs Truce, Break for Huawei, Bloomberg.com [Politics] https://www.bloom-berg.com/news/articles/2019-06-29/xi-trump-agree-to-restart-trade-talk...

6   David, Javier E., (June 24, 2018) @ TeflonGeek, Trump issues challenge to trading partners: Bring down barriers or face 'reciprocity', https://www.cnbc.com/2018/06/24/trump-challenges-trading-partners-on-trade-barriers.html

7   The Globe and Mail (published October 1, 2018 – updated June 20, 2019) NAFTA vs. USMCA: The new North American trade deal explained, https://www.theglobeandmail.com/politics/article-nafta-usmca-trade-deal-explainer-canada-...

8   Petras, George (October 1, 2018) From NAFTA to USMCA: Key changes on trilateral trade pact, *USA Today*, https://www.usatoday.com/story/news/2018/10/01/comparison-nafta-and-usmca-trade-agreements/14871...

9   Navarro, Peter (March 13, 2019) [Opinion] Peter Navarro: President Trump's trade policies make great strides, http://www.usatoday.com/story/opinion/2019/03/13/trump-trade-policies-make-great-strides-peter-navar...

Chapter 6

Trump's Unpredictable International Relations

Trump is not the "ogre" we Americans were told he would be. He has completely confounded and confused the left. Nearly every time the demented Democrat Party thinks President Trump will fall on his sword, at any minute, he issues another tweet which sends them into a mental spiral accompanied by panic attacks, and they begin screaming for impeachment, while wailing, weeping, and the gnashing of teeth. It usually takes about 24 hours for these loony lefties and the lazy leftist "news" outfits to recover from one of his electronic salvos. Most of the time those digital daggers are direct hits, and these anti-Americans end up looking sheepish, foolish, and stupefied. These mentally deficient socialists are fascinating to watch. Though television is considered to be a *cool* medium in the grand scheme of communications, observing these people as they stew in their own hot discombobulation, causes one to sit down on the couch with a bowl of popcorn and an ice-cold beverage for an evening of pleasureful and comical entertainment.

The boldness and brashness of Trump has caused the leaders of other nations to experience cognitive dissonance, because they find themselves agreeing to do things, he has requested, to be in conflict with what their normal behavior has been in the past. They have been used to U.S. presidents requiring little to nothing of them, while they exploit the generosity of America to the utmost degree. Some of them were openly and mildly shocked when President Trump told them to pay their fair share to the North Atlantic Treaty Organization (NATO). Some even said that they had never been asked to pay the agreed upon amount for which that respective country was responsible. That, in and of itself, shows just how much America has been taken for granted, and the president will have no more of it. The fact is each of the countries of NATO have agreed to pay at least two percent of the GDP for the purpose of defense costs.

Any amount less than that is unacceptable. An agreement is an agreement. Table 1 clearly shows who is paying their way and who is failing to live up to the commitment.

So far, it appears that some countries are paying attention to President Trump's urging by paying more of the fair share owed to NATO. It's still early but optimism seems to be in order. As depicted in Table 1, it is obvious that the United States is paying more than it should. The U.S. has been carrying NATO for its 70 years of existence. Trump's position on this matter is straight forward, that is, it's not so much most NATO members are not and have not been paying the appropriate current amount, but what about all of the past years? It is fair to say that these NATO members are in serious arears. To use a home mortgage analysis, how would the lender react if the homeowner had not paid the full mortgage payment? Would interest by charged? Would there be an assessed penalty? At some point, would the homeowner have to pay the full outstanding amount? These questions are not only rhetorical or hyperbolic but quite realistic.

Table 1

Defense Expenditures of NATO Countries of 2018[1]

North Atlantic Treaty Organization (NATO)	Percent of GDP Paid by Member Countries
United States of America	**3.5%**
United Kingdom	**2.1%**
France	1.80%
Germany	1.20%
Italy	1.20%
Canada	1.20%
Turkey	1.70%
Spain	0.90%

Netherlands	. . . .	1.40%
Poland	. . . .	**2.00%**
Norway	. . . .	1.60%
Belgium	. . . .	.090%
Greece	. . . .	**2.30%**
Romania	. . . .	1.90%
Denmark	. . . .	1.20%
Portugal	. . . .	1.40%
Czech Republic	. . . .	1.10%
Hungary	. . . .	1.10%
Slovak Republic	. . . .	1.20%
Lithuania	. . . .	1.90%
Bulgaria	. . . .	1.60%
Croatia	. . . .	1.30%
Latvia	. . . .	**2.00%**
Estonia	. . . .	**2.10%**
Slovenia	. . . .	1.00%
Luxembourg	. . . .	.060%
Albania	. . . .	1.20%
Montenegro	. . . .	1.60%

It's time for NATO to carry its own weight. As a businessman, that is President Trump's position. In essence, the leaders of these countries actually respect Trump, but they also fear him because of the historical power and leadership of America on the world stage.

World Leader Relationships

It did not take long for the president to get the attention of both our allies and our adversaries. They had expected to see the first woman president of the U.S.A. take over the helm of America, and that she, Hillary Rodham Clinton, would resume the status quo of past presidents of America. They were about as shell-shocked as the left-wing misguided media of the U.S.A. when Trump trounced this delusional woman who actually believed that she *deserved* the presidency and has since done all that was possible to try to overthrow the Trump presidency.

President Trump hastened to build and maintain relationships around the world with all of our allies. One of the first leaders he sought to have a quality diplomatic relationship was Prime Minister Theresa May of the United Kingdom and later Boris Johnson.

Theresa May and Boris Johnson

Trump immediately set about to work with Theresa May. From afar, their relationship seemed rather rocky at first, but as time marched on, she and President Trump appeared to work more closely with each other on matters of mutual interest. In fact, when Prime Minister May resigned, the president was quite complimentary of her. It was almost as though he preferred that she stay. May was against the idea of Brexit regarding the world order and the European Union (EU), but President Trump was very supportive of the people of Britain and their decision to disassociate themselves from the EU. He never wavered on that issue, but Prime Minister May resigned because of it. She failed to negotiate a deal regarding the exit from the EU.[2] In the final analysis, a more conservative leader will probably be able to more effectively abide by the will of the British people.

Apparently, the more conservative leader is Boris Johnson who succeeded Theresa May as prime minister in July of 2019. He is considered by some citizens of Great Britain to be the Donald Trump of their country. His intent is to remove his country from the grips of the European Union. He believes that to be the wish of the citizens of his great country, because they voted to do just that, but globalists have resisted the exit of Britain from the EU with great intensity. Johnson, a Tory conservative, seems to have much in common with Trump and expressed a desire to meet with the president on a potential trade deal between the U.S. and the U.K.

Justin Trudeau

Prime Minister of Canada, Justin Trudeau, has had an on-again off-again relationship with President Trump. Early on, Trudeau told President Trump one thing to his face and quite another after Trump departed. Later, Trump said that Trudeau was dishonest and weak. That is not a good way to forge diplomacy. It is highly likely that Trudeau's youth and limited experience, especially as the chief executive of Canada, was the reason for this faux pas. As time moved forward, it appeared so did their personal and professional relationships. The trade agreement USMCA, which replaced NAFTA, seemed to have naturally brought them together since a mutual economic interest was at stake. According to Kevin Liptak of CNN, "Trudeau wants to 'broaden the conversation' with Trump: US and Canadian officials say the relationship has improved."[3] Both of these men fully understand the importance of neighbors being good neighbors. That mutual reality should win the day. Although, no one should be naïve enough to believe that their differences will not result in future disagreements. After all, world leaders are just as human as anyone else. The U.S. and Canada have an awful lot in common, and Canadian and American citizens historically have had a high-quality relationship; therefore, it is very likely that citizens in neighboring countries will not allow two contentious leaders to sour a longstanding friendship.

Presidents of Mexico

When President Trump came into office in January of 2017, he had already issued many derogatory statements about Mexico during his campaign for the presidency. He made it abundantly clear that **President Enrique Peña Nieto of Mexico** and previous leaders had done little to nothing in working with a resolution to the U.S. immigration problem America had been experiencing for decades. Of course, President Nieto objected strenuously. In a prepared speech to the citizens of Mexico Nieto said, "If your recent statements are the result of frustration due to domestic policy issues, to your laws or to your Congress, it is to them that you should turn to, not to Mexicans.

We will not allow negative rhetoric to define our actions. We will only act in the best interest of Mexicans."[4] Based on the comments of both of these presidents, they obviously had significant differences. Their contentious relationship continued until Mexico's new chief executive took over on December 1, 2018.

That is when the left-leaning **Andrés Manuel Lopez Obrador** became Mexico's 58th president. It was generally concluded by most that President Trump and President Obrador would not work well together, but so far, that has not been entirely true. It appears that economic issues seem to have eclipsed personalities and political philosophy. According to President Obrador, "We are proposing investment in productive projects and in job creation, and not only that, also work visas for Mexico and for the United States." He went on to add, "We are in constant communications, and the communication is good."[5] The fact is that President Obrador has been receptive to the needs of the U.S. relative to the broken U.S. immigration system. It was *he* who ordered 6,000 of his troops to Mexico's southern border to slow down the illegal immigration into his country. It was *he* who ordered 15,000 troops to the Mexican northern border to help stem the tide of illegal immigration into the U.S. At this point, it certainly bodes well for a quality relationship between Presidents Trump and Obrador. Hopefully, they will continue to work together on matters of mutual interest such as the USMCA.

Thus far, with the exception of the United Kingdom, only countries of close geographical proximity to the U.S. have been discussed. Although, the U.S. has many allies around the world. One such country is France; wherein, the U.S. has much in common and a rich history. That nation has supported America in war and America has supported it in war. A solid diplomatic relationship is strongly desired and expected for the near and distant future.

President Emmanuel Macron of France

President Macron, like Prime Minister Justin Trudeau of Canada, is youthful and outspoken. Of course, President Trump can be wildly outspoken, opinionated, and forceful in his political positions. Though he and Macron do not always agree on certain issues, they seem to have a genuine, respectful, and personal like for each other. President Trump's visits to France seem to have impressed him. He seemed to truly enjoy the festivities of Bastille Day. President Macron said, "The United States is our friend—nothing will ever separate us." President Trump summed it up as follows, "France is America's first and oldest ally. America and France will never be defeated or divided."[6]

That friendship and relationship was put to the test when President Macron visited the White House a year later. President Trump had a formal state visit and welcomed Macron with a 21-gun salute and a formal dinner at Mount Vernon. On June 1, 2017, President Trump withdrew the U.S. from the Paris Climate Accord of 2015, and writers like Timmons Roberts of the BROOKINGS [PlanetPolicy] issued a dire warning about the terrible thing the U.S. did.[7] His article had the appearance of a frightened school child which was filled with hysteria. With that in mind, more than likely, President Macron expected it to be an uphill slog to convince President Trump to leave the John Kerry-Barack Obama Iran Nuclear Agreement in place. Macron knew that leaders in Europe and the United Kingdom were counting on him; however, he was dealing with a highly skilled and seasoned negotiator with principles who puts America first.[8] Of course, President Trump is a man of his word, and he had promised the American people that he would tear up the Iran agreement because it was not in the best interest of America. Consequently, he soundly rejected this poorly negotiated deal and withdrew the U.S. from this dastardly agreement. Despite that President Macron supported the climate change hoax agreement of Paris, as well as the Iran disaster agreement, and yet he and President Trump still seem to have a good personal relationship unlike that of Angela Merkel of Germany.

Angela Dorothea Merkel Chancellor of Germany

Even during Trump's campaign, he often mentioned the massive hordes of Muslim and Middle East invaders which were awash in Germany, and he laid the fault of that squarely at the feet of Angela

Merkel. Until this occurred, he more or less had a favorable opinion of her as a leader, but this unfettered immigration issue reshaped his view of the woman who was the head of the German government. In effect, Germany became the gateway to Europe for migrants from countries all over the Middle East, Asia, and Africa. In 2015, Germany recorded its highest number (two million) of immigrants in post war history.[9] It is pure speculation, but President Trump has roots in Germany, and it calls into question if his ancestry played a role in the shaping of his views of current German leadership. Now, we know that President Trump's grandfather, Friedrich Trump, was born in a little hamlet called Kallstadt in southwestern Germany where many of his distant relatives still live.[10] Since President Trump is a proud man, it only seems reasonable that he is proud of his German heritage, just as he is about his Scottish ancestry; although, WW II left unsightly pocks upon Germany.

From the interactions of Trump and Merkel, it is obvious that their relationship is somewhat cool. Early on in the Trump presidency, he was not demonstrably supportive of Angela Merkel. In fact, at a meeting in the White House with cameras clicking and rolling, there was a rather awkward moment in which President Trump had an opportunity to shake her hand, but he didn't. Even though things seemed frosty between the two, each of them publicly stated their meeting had been very good.[11] President Trump saw what illegal immigration was doing to America, and he resented that she was doing little to nothing to stem the tide of migrants who were overrunning, and in his words, "ruining" Germany. From the moment President Trump took over, he was intent on straightening out the broken immigration system of the USA. One of the first things that needed to be done was to erect a powerful wall between the USA and Mexico, and that he is still working on to this day. He continues to try to get a delusional democrat-controlled House to write legislation which would correct the errors of the past, but they have no intention of ever changing a thing, because they don't want borders of any kind. In their demented minds they want everyone from everywhere to become *residents* of America, which is ludicrous and idiotic.

Insofar as Germany is concerned, President Trump believes that the invasion of that country by peoples from other nations will dilute the Germanic nature of the populous; thereby, destroy what the proud German people have built, and for that he sees Angela Merkel as a prime mover. In essence, he doesn't believe that she is serving her constituency well. It has become widely known that Chancellor Merkel no longer has the support she once enjoyed by the German people. It appears as though she and President Trump will continue to retain a cordial relationship—but not much more. Besides, Germany is still in arrears regarding the NATO dues. That being said, Germany is an important ally and trading partner; therefore, economics will probably rule the day going forward.

President Moon Jae-in of South Korea

Presidents Trump and Moon of South Korea have sustained positive dialogue all along. Trump has been upfront with Moon on a number of issues, especially trade. President Trump has not liked the disproportional trade deficit in favor of South Korea and has negotiated with President Moon to his (Trump's) satisfaction. Grave matters such as the threat to the citizens of Seoul (more than 11 million people) and the 28,000 U.S. troops along the DMZ, which is posed by Kim Jong Un of North Korea remains to be of great concern.[12] There are many batteries of guns trained upon Seoul at all times, and that is one of the reasons President Trump has worked diligently to try to broker a deal with Kim Jong Un—so many lives at stake. With the recent rather impromptu meeting with Kim Jong Un at the DMZ, there is some hope for a tiny ray of optimism. Insofar as diplomatic relations with Presidents Trump and Moon, they seem to work with each other in an acceptable manner.

Prime Minister Shinzo Abe of Japan

President Trump and Prime Minister Abe, from all outward appearances, have a sound diplomatic, professional, and personal relationship. On more than one occasion, they have played golf together at the Mar-a-Lago Club or at one of President Trump's other courses in northern Virginia. Of course, if one should have read about their golf outings, business meetings, or dinners in say, the *New York Times* or *Washington Post*, you would have primarily read either fake news or at the very least clearly biased diatribe and innuendo against President Trump. In conducting research for this book, as the author, I was amazed at how deluded these two sources, among many others in the media, can really be. To illustrate my point, on May 24, 2019, two writers for the *New York Times* penned this over the top piece "For Trump's Japan Trip, Abe Piles on the Flattery. But to What end?"[13] The article contained the following.

> *When Melania Trump's 49th birthday fell during Mr. Abe's visit to Washington last month, the prime minister and his wife, Akie Abe, were all invited to the cake cutting.*
>
> *So, to keep close ties with Mr. Trump—Mr. Abe's occasional golf buddy and the world leader on the other end of more than 40 discussions or visits since the 2016 election, according to White House officials—the prime minister has planned a visit dripping in a level of ceremony that money can't buy.*
>
> *All of Mr. Abe's plans are meant to remind Mr. Trump, the leader of Japan's most important ally, not to forget about his closest friend in Asia.*

This is not only insulting and condescending to President Trump, but what about Prime Minister Abe? Abe, like Trump, is a successful and proud man of distinction, and yet, this "article" makes them sound cheap and of little consequence—just two old golf buddies having a good time at the expense of their respective countries with little regard for pomp and circumstance. Is it any wonder President Trump considers the *New York Times* to be a purveyor of fake news? It would be easy to provide a similar example from the *Washington Post*; but one egregious example is enough.

In finality, we can conclude that President Trump and Prime Minister Abe can and do work well together on the world stage. This is not to say that they don't have differences. For example, President Trump is insisting the trade deficit of $68 billion between the U.S. and Japan be reduced, and that is something President Abe must resolve. Not to mention, he has promised that Japan will invest $40 billion in automobile infrastructure in the U.S., but that won't suffice for President Trump. The deficit will still have to be reduced. Not only that, but President Trump still insists that Japan play a greater role in its military defense. Of course, two powerful leaders are not always going to agree on everything, but Trump and Abe seem to know how to work things out.

Prime Minister John Scott Morrison of Australia

President Trump met with Prime Minister Morrison at the G20 conference held in Osaka, Japan where international trade and economic issues were front and center during meetings and dinner with allies such as Australia, which was a far cry from Morrison's predecessor, Malcom Turnbull. Morrison recounted and reiterated the close relationship between the USA and Australia of more than 100 years. During the dinner meeting, the president discussed his concerns about deficits with allies and friends. Prior to the dinner, President Trump and Prime Minister Morrison met for more than an hour in positive discussions regarding the two nations and even posed for a picture together.[14] It appears that the two men have a quality relationship going forward.

Thus far, only allies have been discussed, but we live on a planet not only of friends but enemies and adversaries. Still, it is important that we strive to have a positive relationship with all nations including Iran, China, North Korea, and Russia. To varying degrees, all four of these countries are problematic. The leadership of the first country to be discussed is Iran.

Ayatollah Ali Khomeini Supreme Leader of Iran

For context, the U.S. has had a terrible relationship with the leaders of Iran for more than four decades—going back to democrat President

Jimmy Carter—who was the second worst president in U.S. history—only Obama was worse. The Iran Hostage Crisis lasted for 444 days in which 52 diplomats and American citizens were captives of the Iranian government. "The American public had grown tired of the daily drama of the crisis as it played out on national television, and President Carter suffered the scorn of the public. Even today, relationships between Iran and the United States are strained due to this incident."[15] Carter was weak and the Iranians knew it. Carter's administration could not even pull off a rescue with helicopters. They tried but it failed miserably which resulted in the loss of military lives which enraged the military leadership.

The hostages were tortured in ways which makes "waterboarding" seem like playing dodge ball. Toward the end, they were blindfolded while having mock executions with rifles trained on them—not to mention the savage beatings they endured on a regular basis. The mindset then is no better today—death to America! The Iranian leaders are as close to being uncivilized anthropoids as possible. They are hellbent on having nuclear weapons of mass destruction, and most civilized nations do not want that to happen, especially Israel and the United States. No part of the Earth will be safe if these barbarians develop deliverable nuclear warheads, and they must be stopped by whatever means necessary.

Iran's Supreme Leader, Ayatollah Ali Khomeini, the second Supreme Leader of the country, is a ruthless barbarian who is determined to see "Little Satan" Israel and the "Great Satan" America vanquished for evermore. As demented and dangerous as he is, if he did have the weaponry, he would use it. Of course, people like John Kerry and Barack Obama didn't seem to have a problem with that. Both of them did what they could to facilitate Khomeini's goal. Kerry "negotiated" the so-called "nuclear deal" which President Trump scrapped, but Obama did his best to ensure that money would be no object by literally sending pallets of cash on airplanes to Iran, as well as providing access to the $150 billion in frozen assets from 1979 just before he left office. Those are the facts and not fabrications. When it comes to diplomatic or any other relationship, where does this put President Trump? Trump is a negotiator, but even he cannot negotiate with a madman, and if Khomeini is not a lunatic, then he and others around him need to refrain from chanting death to America and stop their full speed ahead momentum toward developing nuclear capability. Even though Iran sponsors terrorism and is number one in the world, I feel certain that President Trump would welcome the opportunity to sit down and talk with Ayatollah Khomeini, but where and under what terms? As things are now, there seems to be nothing but vitriol coming from Tehran, and President Trump continues to increase sanctions on Iran.

> *President Donald Trump imposed sanctions on Iran's supreme leader, Ayatollah Ali Khamenei, and eight senior military commanders, a provocative step designed to increase pressure on the Islamic Republic. Trump told reporters at the White House on Monday that the penalties would deny Khamenei and his office access to financial resources.*[16]

Later, in the article cited above, President Trump said, "The Supreme leader of Iran is the one who ultimately is responsible for the hostile conduct of the regime." It's highly doubtful that Trump is going to blink and more than likely Khomeini will remain steadfast and vehemently opposed to capitulation to the USA. If the sanctions work, the Iranian leadership is in serious trouble; however, the planet is replete with cheaters such as China, Russia, and North Korea. If those countries keep Iran afloat, sanctions will become impotent; and we know that China is already guilty of purchasing oil from Iran, and this could jeopardize trade talks between the U.S. and Beijing.[17] Unfortunately, and sadly, the people who are usually hurt the most by sanctions are the powerless citizens. In this case, the Iranian people will continue to suffer greatly.

President Xi Jinping of the People's Republic of China

From all indications, over the past couple of years, President Trump and President Xi Jinping have what is a "good" personal relationship on the international stage, but they have a lot of room for disagreement, and they do. The unacceptable trade deficit in favor of China has gone on for many years, at about $300 billion annually, and as a result, the United States has practically built the Chinese economy, which has drained America's wealth by at least $5 trillion. This has a direct impact upon the GDP growth rate of the U.S. The facts are, until President Trump came along, our past presidents have done nothing about the trade deficit. They have ignored what the deficits have done to America, concentrating primarily on cheap labor and cheap products.

In addition, the level of intellectual property theft by China is unprecedented. If an American company wants to do business in China, they have to forgo the proprietary guarded secrets of the company and the state-run Chinese companies, as well as the military, have access to this information. If a company wants to do business with China, that is its modus operandi. Personally, I had brief negotiations with a Chinese operative regarding some of my publications, and it didn't take long for me to realize that what I had published was soon available to the Chinese public for which I have never even received a penny. We discussed at length by phone over a period of about three weeks the books he was going to purchase, but it was all just a ruse. Of course, the Chinese have not restricted themselves to just products, they are making significant inroads into the world of technology. "More recently the Chinese theft of intellectual property has risen to new and more sophisticated levels, aimed not simply at "products" but at the U.S. technology base and in an effort to make China the world technology leader.[18] Trade and intellectual property theft are going to prove quite challenging for these two leaders for them to maintain at least a cordial relationship. President Trump is for America first, and President XI is all about China first. Where this all is headed, we shall see.

Kim Jong Un Head of State of North Korea

Kim Jong Un only recently received the title of Head of State of North Korea. The fact is he *is* and has been a ruthless, cruel, and some would say, evil dictator from the beginning. I must be a bit sarcastic, but perhaps a marketing firm from Madison Avenue is trying to help him improve his well-earned very tarnished image. We know of some of the terrible things he's done. We know that he has been starving his people so that he can become a proud owner of a nuclear weapon. We know that he's had people murdered, even some in his own family. If we know these things, can you imagine what horrible things he is doing or has done about which we don't know?

When President Trump announced that he would meet with Un in Singapore, the left went berserk. Their unbridled invectives and condemnation went on for days. According to the delusional Democrat Party, Trump was a horrible person for even suggesting that he would embarrass the nation by meeting with this evil dictator. This type of thinking is counterintuitive to President Trump. He is a negotiator. How can he negotiate anything if he refuses to meet with this dictator? Trump believes in dialogue, and unless he could meet face-to-face with the leader of this rogue nation, how can or would anything positive ever change between North Korea and the U.S.—and the world at large.

Though many critics were dismissive of the meeting afterward, indicating that it was very disappointing and that nothing had been accomplished. How can anyone can be sure of that? Whether any of us like it or not, Kim Jong Un will probably be in charge of Korea for a very long time. The man is in his mid-thirties, and it is highly improbable that anyone will be replacing him in the near or distant future. We must not forget that his grandfather and his father before him were leader-dictators of North Korea.

The critics of Trump did not stop him from working on a second summit in Hanoi, Vietnam. His desire was to continue a dialogue, and in February of 2019, they had another meeting, but President Trump, after two days, pulled the plug on it because he did not see progress being made. Kim Jong Un was insistent that the U.S. lift all sanctions against North Korea first, and then denuclearization could move forward, but that was not an option. As a result, the meeting was abreivated.[19] This was not expected, but as President Trump said, "Sometimes you have to walk." At that point, there was a collective sigh of disappointment about the situation, and many wondered if or when the talks would ever resume.

President Trump being the unpredictable leader that he is, decided an impromptu meeting with Kim Jong Un, after his G20 meeting in Osaka, Japan, could happen. To that end, he reached out to Chairman

Un to test the waters. Since he was in the "neighborhood" so to speak, he wanted to know if Un would like a visit from him. Much to his delight, Kim Jong Un was quite receptive to this unplanned meeting with President Trump. As a result, President Trump met Un at the DMZ which divides North Korea and South Korea. President Trump actually stepped onto North Korean soil. He became the first sitting President of the United States to enter North Korea.[20] Of course, leftist democrats and others thought that was a terrible thing for a U.S. president to do. If any of these critics could boast of any intellectual acuity, they would not take such foolish positions. Trump is trying to build a relationship with a young, ruthless dictator. He's wants to work with Un on *denuclearization*, because Kim Jong Un is not going away anytime soon. Rather than question and condemn President Trump for taking such an action, we should praise him for making such a gutsy move. Hopefully, this might, someday, result in a better life for the more than 25 million starving North Korean citizens, not to mention a safer and more prosperous world.

President Vladimir Vladimirovich Putin of Russia

President Vladimir Putin of Russia is an interesting person. He was born in Leningrad, Russia, U.S.S.R. [now St. Petersburg, Russia] to typical Russian parents October 7, 1952, and projects a tough-guy image to the world.[21] He's reminiscent of the Jimmie Cagney or Edward G. Robinson movie gangster of the 1930s and 1940s in America. The primary difference is Cagney and Robinson were movie actors, but Putin is not acting. Though his formal title is president, he is in practice a cunning and ruthless dictator. Putin is not a man to cross. There are a multitude of stories about his dangerous behaviors. It is well known that he was a KGB (Committee for State Security) agent for 15 years who rose to the rank of lieutenant colonel before he entered into the world of Russian politics. He is not a tall and physically imposing leader. Supposedly, his actual height is five-feet, seven-inches.[22] Some would say he has a Napoleonic Complex. That being said, he is well-trained in martial arts, and even at the age of 64, my guess is he can handle himself quite well, but he doesn't rely on physicality to get things done. He is a devious, treacherous, strong man who can order whatever he wants.

It has become common knowledge that Russia does it's best to meddle in the political system of America, and 2015-2016 was not unusual. That rogue nation has been inserting itself into the affairs of countries for many years. They do all they can to create instability around the world. In the case of the 2016 presidential election, they succeeded beyond their wildest dream. Of course, they had the help of America's delusional Democrat Party, because what was a feeble attempt by the Russians initially became a full-blown investigation and witch hunt in an attempt to create havoc in the U.S. political system. It was not about helping Donald Trump become president. They preferred the notorious Hillary Clinton, because they knew she was an airheaded status quo advocate. Putin has not forgotten the amateurish red "reset button" Clinton tried to make work when she was Secretary of State in 2009 as a gift to Foreign Minister Lavrov. She, Obama, and Biden looked like buffoons. Hillary said, "We worked hard to get the right Russian word. Do you think we got it?" She asked Lavrov, laughing.

"You got it wrong," said Lavrov, as both diplomates laughed. "It should be *perezagruzka* [the Russian word for reset] said Lavrov, "This says *peregruzka* which means overcharged."[23]

At the time, Putin was keenly aware of the dilettante attempts at diplomacy by this triumvirate of stooges. For anyone to even suggest that Putin wanted Clinton to become the U.S. president is ludicrous. Putin knew about businessman Donald Trump, and he knew that Trump was a highly intelligent scrapper in the business world, and he also knew that if Trump should become president, he would have to contend with another smart tough-guy on the world stage. That he didn't relish.

In regards to Russian election meddling, it was reported that at a meeting Obama had admonished Putin to "Knock it off." That must have really jarred Putin, because he had no respect for Obama and he saw him as inept and weak. In June of 2019 President Trump and Putin were together at the G2 meeting and the press puppets badgered President Trump incessantly like panting dogs needing to go outside about telling Putin to stop meddling in our elections. Finally, "Trump turned to Putin and wagged his finger with a smile [saying] 'Don't meddle in the election, president,' Trump said as cameras clicked and reporters shouted questions."[24] This is another example of the president's humor. He knew Putin was going to do his usual foolishness. He also knew that Putin loves Putin, and he is not about to start any type of conflict which might lead to nuclear disaster. Putin has an awesome lavish lifestyle, and he is not about to put that in jeopardy. Old habits are hard to break, and Putin's days as a KGB agent are still a fresh memory.

Never underestimate President Trump. He knows the kind of man with whom he is dealing, and he also knows that Putin is not going to take any overt action which might result in the destruction of Russia or America, and the president also knows that energy has been a tool of Russia used to behaviorally affect the citizens of Europe. Chapter 7 deals with energy and U.S. independence.

————

Endnotes

1   Feldman, Sarah (April 1, 2019) Defense Expenditures of NATO Countries, https://www.statista.com/chart/17529/nato-defense-spending/
2   Starspost (May 30, 2019) Why did Theresa May resign as Prime Minister and how will it affect the Brexit deal? https://starspost.com/why-did-theresa-may-resign-as-prime-minister-and-how-will-it-affect-...
3   Liptak, Kevin (June 20,2019) Trudeau wants to 'broaden the conversation' with Trump: US and Canadian officials say relationship has improved, https://www.Cnn.com/2019/06/20/politics/Trudeau-trump-us-canada-meeting/index.html
4   Hansler, Jennifer [CNN] (April 6, 2018) Mexican President to Trump: 'Nothing and no one stands above the dignity of Mexico, https://www.cnn.com/2018/04/06/politics/Enrique-pena-nieto-trump-border-responsive/index...
5   Birnbalm, Emily (December 5, 2018) Mexico's new president says relationship with Trump is 'good' expects immigration talks soon, *The Hill*, https://thehill.com/latino/419867-new-mexican-president-says-relationship-with-trump-is-...
6   Bhatti, J. & Onyanga-Omara, J. (July 14, 2017) Paris puts on a dazzling Bastille Day display for President Trump, *USA TODAY*, https://www.usatoday.com/story/news/world/2017/07/14/president-trump-bastille-day/478421001/
7   Roberts, Timmons BROOKINGS [PlanetPolicy] (June 1, 2018) One year since Trump's withdrawal from the Paris climate agreement, https://www.brookings.edu/blog/planetpolicy/201806/01/one-year-since-trumps-withdraw...
8   Fontemaggi, Francesco [AFP] (April 22, 2018) Can Macron's White House visit save the Iran deal? https://news.yahoo.com/macons-white-house-visit-save-iran-deal-022435661.html
9   DW News, Two Million: Germany records largest influx of immigrants in 2015,https://www.dw.com/en/two-million-germany-records-largest-influx-of-immigrants-in-201 ...

10 McGrane, Sally (April 29, 2016) The Ancestral Home of the Trumps, *The NewYorker*, https://www.newyorker.com/culture/culture-desk/the-ancestral-German-home-of-the-trumps

11 Williams, Richard A.L. (March 17, 2017) Donald Trump refuses to shake AngelaMerkels's hand [The Independent]https://www.independent.co.uk/news/world/Americas/us-politics/Donald-trump-angela-mer...

12 Brook, Tom Vanden (June 5, 2018) Pentagon bases about 28,000 U.S. Troops in South Korea, *USATODAY*, https:www.usatoday.com/story/news/politics/2018/06/05/u-s-bases-28-000-troops-south-korea-summit...

13 Rogers, K. & Rich, M. (May 24, 2019) For Trump's Japan Trip, Abe Piles on the Flattery. But to what end? *The New York Times*, https://www.nytimes.com/2019/05/24/us/politics/trump-japan-abe-flattery.html

14 ABC NEWS (June 27, 2019) Scott Morrison meets with Donald Trump over dinner in Japan ahead of G20 Summit, https://www.abc.net.au/news/2019/-06-28/scott-morrison-meets-with-donald-trump-at-din...

15 West, Doug (October 4, 2018) The Iran Hostage Crisis: 1979 to 1981 [Owlcation]https://owlcation.com/humanities/The-Iran-Hostage-Crisis-1979-to-1981

16 Saleha, M., Pettypiece, S., & Wainer, D. (June 24, 2019) Trump Sanctions Iran's Supreme Leader in Provocative Move, [Politics] Bloomberg, https://www.bloomberg.com/news/articles/2019-06-24/trump-says-he-is-imposing-sanctio...

17 Hayek, Jim (July 14, 2019) Report: U.S. Weighing Sanctions Against China for Buying Oil from Iran, [American Truth Today] https://americantruthtoday.com/politics/2019/07/14/report-u-s-weighing-sanctions-against-china-for-buying-oil-from-iran/?utm_source=sprkist&utm_ca...

18 Gallington, D., & Wagner, A. (February 5, 2019) Taking on China's intellectual property theft, *Washington Times*, https://washingtontimes.com/news/2019/feb/5/taking-on-chinas-intellectual-property...

19 Jackson, David (February 28, 2019) Donald Trump, Kim Jong Un fail to strike deal, call off nuclear weapons talks early, *USA TODAY*,

https://www.usatoday.com/story/news/politics/2019/02/28/ Donald-trump-kim-jong-un-nuclear-Vietnam-s...

20 Stokols, Eli and Kim, Victoria (June 29, 2019) Trump meets Kim Jong Un at DMZ and becomes first sitting U.S. president to enter North Korea, *Los Angeles Times*, [politics], https://www.latimes.com/politics/ la-na-pol-trump-korea-dmz-Kim-moon-20190630-story.h...

21 *Encyclopedia Britannica*, Vladimir Putin, https://www. britannica.com/Vladimir-Putin

22 CNN [AnswersAfrica], How Tall is Vladimir Putin and Other Facts About The Russian President, https://answersafrica.com/ how-tall-is-putin-other-facts.html

23 Dougherty, Jill [CNN Foreign Affairs Correspondent] (March 6, 2009) Clinton 'reset button' gift to Russian FM gets lost in translation, http://politicalticker.blogs.cnn.com/2009/03/06/ Clinton-reset-button-gift-to-russian-fm-gets...

24 Fritz, John & Jackson, David (June 29, 2019) Trump defends his exchange withVladimir Putin over election meddling, *USATODAY*, https://www.usatoday.com/Story/news/politics/2019/06/29/ Donald-trump-vladimir-putin-election-meddli...

Chapter 7

ENERGY: A Piece of the Trump Puzzle

At the outset, Donald Trump knew that energy was a very important part of the make America great again puzzle. He and America had watched, throughout the Obama administration, an intentional destruction of America's energy capability and potential. Obama became a firewall against the progress of energy. He did his best to prevent oil drilling and fought every attempt which would allow the opening of pipelines for oil, natural gas, or any form of energy production, including and especially coal. This is not rhetorical ranting or hyperbole. It is disgusting. This is the unvarnished truth.

It is important to get a sense of the thinking of President Trump, and that can be accomplished by examining some of his publicly stated thinking and philosophy.

End the war on beautiful clean coal – State of the Union Address 1-30-2018

Represent Pittsburgh, not Paris: Coal over climate agreement – NPR-Fact-check on 2017 Trump administration promises, 6-2-2017

Revive the coal industry: end efforts to curb carbon- *NYT* – 3-28-2017

Stop threatening the livelihood of our coal miners – State of the Union address to Congress – 2-28-2017

Fracking will lead to American energy independence – 2016 AFA action iVoter Guide on 2016 presidential hopefuls – 11-8-2016.

EPA is killing energy companies – Second 2016 Presidential Debate at Washington University – 10-9-2016

Focus on disease & clean water, not "climate change" –
ScienceDebate.org: 20 questions for 2016 presidential race – 10-9-2016

America invested in solar panels and it was a disaster –
First 2016 presidential debate at Hofstra University – 9-26-2016

Green energy is just an expensive feel-good for tree-huggers – *Crippled America* by Donald Trump, p.63-11-3-2015

We have 2 trillion barrels of oil; enough for 283 years –
Crippled America, by Donald Trump, p.63 – 11-3-2015

Offered to oversee response to 2010 Gulf of Mexico oil spill – politico.com article with Trump's "Never Enough" biographer – 9-25-2015

Wind energy projects are industrial monstrosities – Never Enough, by Michael D'Antonio, p.318 – 9-22-2015

This is only a partial listing of President Trump's positions on energy and oil. For a more complete listing, review [OnTheIssues] which can be found at http://www.ontheissues.org/Celeb/Donald_Trump_Energy_+_Oil.htm.[1]

It is clear that President Trump has his own ideas, thoughts, and personal philosophy about U.S. energy sources and does not mince words about his positions. This is a refreshing experience, because most people who seek political office seem to have one opinion on one day and another on a different day. They tend to be more like moving targets than stationary objects. Trump does not recoil; he will double down, and if necessary, triple down. He backs down from no one. If a fight is picked with him, then that's exactly what will happen. In the article cited above, the president is brutally candid about the prospects of solar energy not making a significant difference in the *short-term*. He is also quite critical of the whole concept of green energy because the breakeven point in investment is too far out to be considered a good investment. This is the businessman in the president taking precedence over emotional responses. Essentially, he thinks for the most part that "climate change" is a hoax; although, he does agree that man might make a small contribution to climate issues, but he soundly rejects the hysteria of the left and the socialist Democrat Party which are basically one and the same. There has been recent research which seems to support Trump's hypothesis of man contributing minimally to the increase in Earth temperature. "A devastating series of research papers has just been published, revealing that human activity can account for no more than a .01% C rise in global temperatures, meaning that all the human activity targeted by radical climate change alarmists—combustion engines, airplane flights, diesel tractors—has virtually no measurable impact on the temperature of the planet."[2] These findings have been replicated at Kobe University in Japan. It's time that the real truth be revealed to all of humanity, and these alarmists of planetary gloom and doom be held accountable for their questionable "scientists" and left leaning academicians who make outlandish claims. Environmental extremists preach and proclaim that the Earth is so precious that it must not be disturbed. This sphere upon which we all reside is here for our use, because God provided it for us.

President Trump is not about to let delusional, ignorant; malcontents stop America from remaining energy independent. He is putting America first. Isn't it obvious that the less we depend on the Middle East for oil the better off this nation is? For decades OPEC held America hostage because of its "black gold." Any thinking person should be able to understand this, but then, there is a dearth of believers who actually believe that former Vice President, Al Gore, actually knows something about climatic conditions. He's not a scientist. He's a former politician who is all washed up; yet, he has become a billionaire as an evangelist for climate change. According to some of his errant prognostications, the world should have ended long ago because of human abuse of the Earth.

Oil Drilling

It cannot be argued that different presidents have differing views about oil drilling. When I lived in Florida, and Jeb Bush was the governor, he found the idea of having oil rigs off the coast to be repugnant, so he called his brother, President George W. Bush, and told him to disallow oil rigs off the coast of Florida, and that's what happened. The rigs would have been about three miles offshore, and it didn't seem to me to ruin the Florida coastline on the east or west coast; however, oil rigs never appeared near Florida shores. By in large, President Bush was supportive of the production of oil, but he nor any of our recent presidents really wanted the U.S. to become energy independent. Since George W. Bush was and is a globalist new world order type, he would have offended worldwide powers. After he left the presidency, this country had the misfortune of electing democrat Barack H. Obama, and he immediately set out to destroy anything and everything which related to America's power and greatness, and oil, coal, and natural gas were casualties of his strategic effort to dismember America. No one should ever say that Obama didn't give it his all, because he did everything he could to cripple this country right up to the last day of his reign of terror over the USA.

Then, seemingly, out of nowhere came a blue-collar billionaire businessman, Donald J. Trump, as President of the United States who saw the world of energy from a completely different viewpoint. He saw a revived America, an exciting America of Roman candles which lit up the sky. His vision was of the great America of the past. The America which was the "shining city on a hill", not the flickering, dying candle fashioned by Obama. Trump's words and actions supported a full out aggressive initiative to drill for oil in as many places as possible; however, with the introduction of wide-spread fracking, some companies appear to be reluctant about putting down new oil rigs offshore.[3] Despite this reticence, the U.S. has proudly become energy independent and self-sufficient in an amazingly short period of time. That has been achieved because oil has only been one very important part of the energy sources. The U.S. natural gas production has increased significantly to the point the U.S. is able to sell the product abroad. The first ever sale of liquefied natural gas went to Poland; thereby, providing an alternative to Russian natural gas. The U.S. has become a competitor in providing natural gas to European countries. "[Russia] will have to rethink their tactics and strategy ... they'll have to consider the United States as an increasing power in the European gas market," the diplomat said.[4] According to the U.S. Energy Information Administration, at least as of 2016, the U.S. has "about 2,462 trillion cubic feet of technically recoverable resources of dry natural gas in the United States . . . to last about 90 years."[5] That number will depend upon the amount imported and exported over time. Natural gas, oil, and geothermal energy have been extracted from the earth by using an old technique commonly called fracking.

Hydraulic Fracking

My guess is most people in our country think that hydraulic fracking is a new methodology or technology, but it is far from that. This is a proven drilling technology which dates back to 1947. "More than 1.7 million U.S wells have been completed using the fracking process, producing more than seven billion barrels of oil and 600 trillion cubic feet of natural gas."[6] As could be expected, the Obama administration issued a rule regarding fracking on BLM land which made it extremely difficult to work with, but when the Trump administration kicked into gear that rule was eliminated and production resumed. To be fair, there are usually two sides to every story. What about the pros and cons of fracking?[7]

Some pros are:
- Access to More Gas and Oil: – can reach to depths which other methods cannot.
- Lower Taxes:-lowering of taxes on essential things like gas and oil.
- Self-dependent: – meaning we must depend less on other nations for energy.
- Better Air Quality:-burning gas causes less carbon dioxide in the atmosphere, and scientifically, carbon dioxide is not a pollutant, it is what we exhale and plants consume to create oxygen.
- Reduced Dependency on Foreign oil:-provides greater national independence.

Some cons are:[8]
- It can pave the way to health problems: wells created through fracking can have methane leaks.

- It can lead to accidents – a Texas incident resulted in vegetation being killed and contaminated the surrounding land, causing homeowners to flee.
- It uses a lot of water – fracking uses a mixture to break shale rocks apart and push gas out.

If the benefits are weighed against potential problems, it is easy to determine that the pros exceed the cons. The truth is the public is generally not well-served by the media about fracking. Since the media aligns itself with environmental extremists, it only stands to reason that biased reporting would occur. It's amazing how leftists can take this old drilling technique and turn it into something controversial in today's world.

General Conclusions Regarding Renewable Energy Sources

There are two prominent concerns, among others, about either solar or wind power. As compared to fossil fuel sources, there is no real contest when it comes to cost and efficacy. Solar power development is still too costly and it can only provide a fraction of energy which is needed to power the U.S. Nevada is a state in which I used to reside (2007-2017) that set a goal of being able to provide 440 megawatts of power to serve more than 100,000 homes by 2020 for the residents of the greater Las Vegas area.[9] I personally watched this solar project crawl across the dry desert lake floor over that 10-year period. The last time I drove by it in 2017, it took ten-minutes, traveling at 65 miles per hour to traverse the entire operation while driving parallel along highway 95. Over many decades, and millions of acres of solar panels splayed out over BLM land across the state, perhaps solar power can become a significant energy source for Nevada, but at this point, fossil fuel will still need to be exploited. This is not to say that solar power should be abandoned, but it is to say that it will take a very long time for it to become a competitive source of energy for Nevada. Nevada is a unique state in many ways. The land which accommodates solar panels isn't very habitable and has very limited uses. Other states, such as those in the northeast or Deep

South are hardly candidates for millions of acres of BLM land which experiences temperatures often in the high triple-digits.

There are a number of problems with wind power. Like solar, it can only produce a very limited amount of energy at this point in time. My first encounter with a wind farm was in 1986. I was driving from a meeting in Palm Desert, California to another business meeting in Hollywood. I had been on the road traveling through the desert for about an hour when I came upon these massive windmill-structures with their long blades splitting the sky for as far as I could see. As I drove, those things seemed to never end. My thoughts were about how hideous they appeared. To me, they were a blight upon the land. I still see them that way; however, they are much more than an eyesore, they emit loud annoying whirring sounds and kill millions of our feathered-avian friends. These monstrosities kill birds of all types— even bald eagles. The numbers of annual kills within the U.S. range from lows to very telling highs. To illustrate, "Wind turbines kill an estimated 140,000 to 328,000 birds each year in North America, making it the most threatening from of green energy."[10] A different source/study concluded that, "A 2013 study published in *The Wildlife Society Bulletin* found that wind turbines killed an estimated 573,000 birds annually in the United States. . .[moreover] the goal is to have these turbines produce 20% of generated electrical energy in the U.S. by 2030 . . . ."[11] That study was six years ago, so obviously with an estimated 50,000 active wind turbines nationwide, and growing, that number has to be significantly higher.

President Trump has been dismissed by the media and others who report on this matter. It seems to be because he had a legal scuffle with officials in Scotland about wind turbines and the unsightliness of them on the coast where he has a Trump International golf course. It should be noted that this occurred before he was elected president. Regardless of what his detractors might say about his motives for criticizing these mammoth machines, the fact is wind power energy only produces about 6% of the power needed in the U.S. Is it worth it? Is it worth destroying so much of our fragile wildlife? Is it worth it to create these unsightly eyesores all over America the beautiful? I find it incredibly hypocritical that leftist liberals complain and whine about the "assault" on the environment on a daily basis, but not one peep out of them about the wanton destruction of innocent birds, including golden and bald eagles. People are fined and incarcerated for the killing of bald eagles; yet, the slaughter of these precious creatures, the national bird, is permissible if an inanimate object such as a wind turbine that splatters their spirited bodies into oblivion while they soar in the air. The average height of one of these current wind turbines is about 212 feet with a blade that spans more than 115 feet and each one sits on more than an acre of land. These things are like giant blenders which crush these fowl like ground laden autumn leaves under the feet of humans. There are new ones coming on line that dwarfs what is currently in use. These are massive imposing structures which will do even more damage.

Older Forms of Energy Sources

Hydropower has been a part of the U.S energy arsenal for nearly 150 years. "On September 30, 1882, the world's first hydroelectric power plant began operation in the Fox River in Appleton, Wisconsin."[12] Since that time, the harnessing of America's waterways has become a major source of clean, renewable energy. Dams across the nation began springing up to meet the demands of its citizens as hydropower gained in popularity. For example, the Hoover Dam, a few miles outside of Las Vegas, came along during the Great Depression. It was initially called the Boulder Dam, but it was finally renamed in honor of President Herbert Hoover (1929-33). It provided work for American citizens at a time when they most needed employment. It not only generates electricity, but it impounds Lake Mead and provides for flood and silt control, agricultural irrigation, and domestic water supply. It is the highest concrete arch dam in the United States.[13] On a personal note, I have visited it many times over the years, and it is an impressive structural marvel.

The Tennessee Valley Authority (TVA) in 1933 "built dams, managed flood control, and soil conservation programs, and more. It greatly boosted the region's economy."[14] Both documentary and dramatic films have been made about this massive U.S government public venture. I recall visiting the Fontana Dam just outside of Bryson City, N.C. in 1980. Though its construction began in 1942, it was not completed until 1944. "The dam is 480 feet high and stretches 2,365 feet across the Little Tennessee River . . . . Fontana Reservoir provides 238 miles of shoreline and 10,230 acres of water surfaces for recreation activities."[15] The area is attractive and very visually appealing.

The Grand Coulee Dam of Washington state "is by far the largest hydroelectric project in the U.S., with an installed capacity of 6,809 [megawatts] (MW). In addition to producing hydroelectric power, the dam also provides water for irrigation projects that span more than 670,000 acres."[16] This dam has improved the lives of residents in the area in many remarkable ways. Though electricity is practically taken for granted, these citizens have enjoyed the benefits of Grand Coulee for many decades. Perhaps, this is the primary reason President Trump has such a positive view of hydropower, because he supports concepts and practices which make the lives of Americans better. According to the U.S. Energy Information Administration, hydropower accounts for 7.0% of U.S. electric energy.[17] This is not to say that there aren't concerns about the use of hydropower, because it can disrupt the ecosystems of rivers, communities, and be problematic for aquatic life such as salmon and other fish life.[18] With that being said, the advantages far outweigh the disadvantages, and it appears that the Trump administration will continue to support the development of hydropower, including geothermal energy.

- Geothermal energy has potential to become a significant provider of electricity. Currently, "The United States leads the world in the amount of electricity generated with geothermal energy. In 2018, there were geothermal power plants in seven states, which produced about 16.7 billion kilowatthours (kWh), equal to 0.4% of total U.S. utility-scale electricity generation."[19] The advantages are: environmental friendly, a renewable source, potential capacity, a stable resource, great for heating/cooling, no fuel required, small land footprint, stable resource, cost competitive in some areas, available in most places, renewable for the next 4 billion years, abundant supply, significant savings for home owners. The disadvantages are: potential emissions, surface stability, high cost of electricity, high up-front costs for heating and cooling systems, location specific, distribution costs, some studies show reservoirs can be depleted, heat pumps need a power source, and may run out of steam.[20] Still, though these disadvantages must be considered, the potential for geothermal power is great. Geothermal, in comparison to solar and wind lags behind in R&D, but that may change in the near future. "Geothermal is a laggard in comparison, but maybe not for long. It looks like the Trump administration is gearing up for a new round of R&D that could propel the US geothermal industry out of the doldrums."[21]

The most controversial energy source is nuclear power which provides for 9.6% of electricity needs of the U.S.[22] Nuclear power has fallen on hard times since the Chernobyl disaster of 1986 in Ukrainian Soviet Socialist Republic where many people died as a result, and the more recent Fukushima Daiichi accident in Japan of 2011. These nuclear failures have, justifiably, caused many to be trepidatious about the future of nuclear energy. Despite this, President-elect Trump, made it clear about his thoughts regarding nuclear energy. He said, "I'm in favor of nuclear energy, very strongly in favor of nuclear energy," adding: "If a plane goes down, people keep flying. If you get into an auto crash, people keep driving."[23] Today, President Trump does what he does best, and that is, he uses common sense. He does not let unfortunate situations, circumstances, and conditions cloud his judgment; therefore, it can be expected that nuclear power will remain as a major source of energy in the United States for the foreseeable future.

To summarize, fossil fuels are clearly the source of energy upon which we must heavily rely for the next several decades. Oil and coal are essential to our survival as a people. This is not a binary choice—fossil or renewable. Even though, there is an abundance of fossil fuels now, there are finite amounts of oil and natural gas beneath the surface of our great country. For the sake of this nation, its citizens, and the world at large, all forms of energy should be used going forward. It is a question of sensibly prioritizing the needs of the nation, and this is what President Trump and his administration supports.

———

Endnotes

1   OnTheIssues [Every Political Leader on Every Issue] Donald Trump on Energy & Oil, http://www.ontheissues.org/Celeb/ Donald_Trump_Energy_+_Oil, htmConservative Society, Climate Change Imploding as New Science Discovers Human Activity Has Zero Impact On Global Temperatures, https:// www.conservativesociety.org/alert/climate-change-imploding-as-new-science-discovers-human-activity-has-zero-impact-on-global-temperature...

2   Conservative Society, Climate Change Imploding as New Science Discovers Human Activity Has Zero Impact On Global Temperatures, https://www.conservativesociety.org/ alert/climate-change-imploding-as-new-science-discovers-human-activity-has-zero-impact-on-global-temperature...

3   Tabuchi, Hiroko & Wallace, Tim (January 23, 2018) Trump Would Open Nearly All U.S. Waters to Drilling. But Will They Drill? *New York Times*, https://www.Nytimes.com/interactive/ 201801/23/climate/trump-offshore-oil-drilling.html

4   Gramer, Robbie (June 8, 2017) First U.S. Natural Gas Shipped to Poland [The Cable] https://foreignpolicy.com/2017/06/08/ first-u-s-natural-gas-shipped-to-poland/

5   American Geosciences Institute (AGI) How much natural gas doe the United States have, and how long will it last?http:// www.americangeosciences.org/critical-issues/faq/how-much-natural-gas-does-unite...

6   Independent Petroleum Association of American (IPAA) Hydraulic Fracturing, https://www.ipaa.org/fracking/

7   Conserve Energy Future, https://www.conserve-energy-future. com/pros-and-cons-of-fracking.php

8   Lombardo, Crystal (February 2, 2016) Pros and Cons of Fracking, [Vision Launch] https://visionlaunch.com/ pros-and-cons-of-fracking/

9   Nevada's Dry Lake Sets Good Model for Solar Energy on Public Lands, https://willderness.org/articles/ blog/nevadas-dry-lake-sets-good-model-solar-energy-...

10 Bryce, Emma (March 16, 2016) Will Wind Turbines Ever Be Safe For Birds? [Audubon] https://www.audubon.org/news/will-wind-turbines-ever-be-safe-birds

11 American Eagle Foundation, Conventional Wind Energy-A Design Deadly for Birds, https://www.eagles.org/take-action/wind-turbine-fatalities/

12 [America's Story from America's Library] The World's First Hydroelectric Power Plant Began Operation September 30, 1882/ http://www.americaslibrary.gov/jb/Gilded/jb_gilded_hydro_1.html

13 Editors of Encyclopedia Britannica, Hoover Dam, https://www.britannica.com/Topic/Hoover-Dam

14 America's Story from America's Library, https://www.americaslibary.gov/jb/gilded/jb_gilded_hydro_3.html

15 TVA – Fontana, https://www.tva.gov/Energy/our-Power-System/Hydroelectric/Fontana-Reservoir

16 The Largest Hydroelectric Power Stations in the United States [World Facts]https://www.worldatlas.com/articles/the-largest-hydroelectric-power-stations-in-the-united...

17 U.S. Energy Information Administration (eia), https://eia.gov/tools/faq.phy?id=427&t=3

18 Nunez, Christina, National Geographic [Reference] Hydropower, Explained, https://www.nationalgeographic.com/environment/globalwarming/hydropower

19 U.S. Energy Information Administration (eia), https://www.eia.gov/energyexplained/index.php?page=geothermal_use

20 Meyers, Glenn (February, 11, 2016) [Planetsave] Geothermal Energy Advantages and Disadvantages, https://planetsave.com/2016/02/11/geothermal-energy-advantages-and-disadvantages/

21 Casey, Tina (January 1, 2018) Trump Holds Geothermal Card Up His Sleeve When Pitching "Energy Dominance", [cleantechnica] https://cleantechnica.com/2018/o1/01/trump-holds-geothermal-card-sleeve-pitching-energy...

22 U.S. Energy Information Administration (eia), https://www.eia.gov/energy/explain/?page=us_energy_home

23 Bajak, Alezu (November 15, 2016) Hopes for Nuclear Power, However Unlikely, Blossom With Trump's Rise [Undark.org] https://undark.org/2016/11/15/donald-trump-nuclear-power/

Chapter 8

The Trump Infrastructure Renewal

In order to appreciate the Trump initiative, we must go back to when Obama announced *his* infrastructure plans in 2009 which, by the way, never really materialized. He made such infrastructure proclamations a total of five times, but his shovel ready jobs never really happened. "In the end, however, only $98.3 billion of the $800 billion stimulus was dedicated to transportation and infrastructure."[1] This was his modus operandi. Tell us one thing, then do another, but he is not President Trump, because Trump is Trump and a man of his word.

Trump has an oxygen depleted mountain to climb, not including a substantial number of F-Rs who despise the Constitution and Declaration of Independence upon which this miraculous nation has stood the test of time. He has to, somehow, convince delusional democrats who have burning hatred for him to climb aboard the Trump Train at least until the next stop. The question is will these blind-haters of the president support any comprehensive infrastructure agreement for the good of the American people? Will they ride the train far enough to make a difference? More succinctly stated, will they do what is right? Even though the president has proposed a plan for a $1.5 trillion infrastructure plan, the democrats seem to remain sidetracked in trying to find a way to oust him from office, so it is highly unlikely that they can or will work with him for any reason.

President Trump's plan is to only use $200 billion initially from direct federal spending and then match state and local governments at a four-to-one ratio as they make investments into infrastructure in order to achieve the $1.5 trillion goal. According to D.J. Gribbin, Trump's special assistant for infrastructure, "What we really want to do is provide opportunities for state and local governments to receive federal funding when they're doing what's politically hard, and increasing investment in infrastructure,"[2] Though this proposal was made in February of 2018, by May of 2019 the Speaker of the

House, Nancy Pelosi (D), and Minority Leader, Chuck Schumer (D), of the Senate began making unsubstantiated claims about President Trump in which he was accused of some type of "coverup". Of course, that did not sit well with the president and talks immediately broke down. He was tired of them going down the investigative track when they needed to go down the track of working with him for infrastructure.[3] He could not see how they could work together as they continued to investigate him for things he did not do.

Overview of Infrastructure Needs

It is without question that the nation's infrastructure has been crumbling for many years. Even the country's interstate highway system has been deteriorating for decades, which was signed into law on June 29, 1956 by President Dwight Eisenhower. The bill created a 41,000-mile "National System of Interstate and Defense Highways."[4] Four years later, I-10 came to my city in Jacksonville, Florida. That was nearly 60 years ago. Since those days, I have traversed the width of this country by automobile on I-10 more than once with the last time being in 2006. On that trip, we encountered portions of that highway which were reminiscent of road conditions in Jamaica, because the roads on that island tend to look like a war zone. If you have ever been to Jamaica, you understand my inference. Crossing Texas was a dangerous and harrowing experience at 85 miles per hour. By the way, that speed limit is posted and approved of by the state of Texas; however, there are patches of I-10 west of Houston which a speed limit of about 55 is probably more apropos. Interstate-10 stretches across America with a, seemingly, innumerable number of "Road Work Ahead" signs, road barrels, and cones from L.A. to Tampa, Florida. Similar conditions exist on I-4, I-5, I-40, I-70, I-75, and I-95. In fact, I've experienced this on nearly every interstate highway I've used in the last 25 years. Just how many repairs of a roadway system is enough after more than 60 years? After all, this system was not built by the Egyptians, Greeks, or Romans who constructed things which lasted for thousands of years. Let's not forget, they built things primarily with two things—human labor and ingenuity; however, it is about time for this highway system and other roads to be reinvigorated, which is what the president and millions of American citizens see as needed and a priority.

It's not only roads, but what about the bridges of America? According to federal data, there are approximately 61,000 bridges throughout the USA which are structurally deficient and in need of repairs, which handle 215 million crossings per day as part of the Interstate Highway System[5.] According to President Trump, "Together, we can reclaim our great building heritage. We will build gleaming new roads, bridges, highways, railways, and waterways all across our land."[6]

In 2017, the American Society of Civil Engineers issued its infrastructure report card on America's overall infrastructure, and it was a D+ with America's dams averaging a D.[7] Dams/dykes and levees in the USA are under constant pressure. By now, most Americans across the nation are aware of the Oroville Dam failure of Oroville, California in February of 2017. It is the tallest earthen dam with a 770-foot face and 901-foot top of the spillway. Even after $1.1 billion was spent to repair it, there are numerous water seepage points trickling and dozens of points along the dam's spillway.[8] This dam clearly needs a more robust repair effort. For that matter so do waterways levees and dams across the nation. Practically, it seems, that New Orleans is under the threat of Lake Pontchartrain nearly every year because of hurricanes like Katrina. I cannot imagine living under the threat of a massive wall of water coming down at any given time, but the citizens seem to sit beneath it without undue concern; even though, it is well known that supporting levees are very vulnerable. The fact is, if Pontchartrain and its levees ever truly give way, within minutes New Orleans and all of its citizens will be swept out to sea. That city and its citizens will no longer be with us. The power of nature's water can be dumbfounding.

What about infrastructure for rail service? We have relied on trains for decades to move products all around in the USA. Admittedly, they do move at a glacial pace but they have made products available to U.S. citizens which otherwise they would not have had. It's really unfortunate that air service has preempted the development of rail and passenger service in the U.S. There was a time when trains were the preeminent form of transportation, but the aircraft industry and their lobbyists put trains on the sidetracks to nowhere long ago, and now what little passenger service that is available can be a miserable experience. In Europe and England, passenger trains run on time but not in America. Other countries such as japan and China have trains which not only run on time but at blistering speeds, and President Trump would like for the U.S. to catch up.

> *The plan calls for creating new high-speed rail lines deep underground—the basic idea behind the English Channel, or Chunnel, that whisks travelers at 186 miles per hour from London to Paris in just two hours and 20 minutes. That's less time than the Amtrack from New York City to Washington, D.C.— even though the two U.S. cites are 40 miles closer.*[9]

President Trump has sought the advice and counsel of such genius inventors as Elon Musk who envisions that the tunnels at some point will be used as a hyperloop which is his idea of moving people and cargo around through a system of giant vacuum tubes.[10] This is all quite Avant-guard, but conceptionally and practically quite achievable, and the president wants to move forward on this type of action.

Where is the Congress and President Trump on all of this? It is up to Congress to appropriate funds for the infrastructure, and the democrat leadership seems to be too busy chasing delusions to concern themselves with the needs of America. Their preoccupation with strawmen and specious nonsense about the removal of the president from office has captivated any productive time which might be available. Congressman Jerry Nadler appears as though he is obsessed if not possessed. Long before Donald Trump became President Trump Nadler and Trump have been sparring with each other for decades, and he usually comes up on the losing end. As a result, Nadler has lost his sense of direction. He has not been able to come to grips with his total failure to incriminate President Trump; yet, he blindly continues on his road of vendetta and personal persecution of the president. Hopefully, voters of the 10th District of New York City are paying attention to Nadler's preoccupation with President Trump when what they really need is intelligent representation. In the midst of this deluded thinking, President Trump has stood tall, firm, confident, and ready to move things forward, but this takes democrats and republicans working together with the president. However, it was reported in the *The Hill* in May of 2018 that the president's infrastructure plan had reached a dead-end. "Rep. Peter DeFazio (D-Ore.), the ranking member of the Transportation and Infrastructure Committee, told *The hill* Wednesday that there has been no movement on a bill with the Chairman Bill Shuster (R-Pa.). . . . "As far as I know, it's been shredded, or burned, or something. It doesn't exist [regarding] the president's rebuilding blueprint."[11] Ordinarily, this type of bill would usually appeal to the Democrat Party, but Donald Trump, a republican, is president; therefore, he is not to be supported or trusted regarding anything. Besides, 2020 is just around the corner, and the democrats cannot allow him to be looked upon by the voting public as a good or even a great president.

Rural Infrastructure

The president and his administration have not left out the needs of rural America. As can be expected, left-wing media sources such as CNBC and the *Washington Post* like to paint pictures of base pandering. For example, one headline of CNBC indicated "A big chunk of an apparent White House infrastructure plan would target Trump's rural base."[12] How childish, insulting, and ignorant. President Trump's so-called "base" includes citizens all across the USA. He could not have won the presidency with only rural America. The *Washington Post* reported that one democrat congressional aide said, "It's no surprise their political base gets the money fast, and everybody else has to beg the administration to support their project."[13] Once again, another childlike and ignorant response is uttered. From the beginning, the message of the president has had great appeal to Americans throughout the land. He is the president of all Americans. For example, there is a need for broadband communications expansion in rural America, and that has been included in the Trump administration plan. The plan is a relatively comprehensive document which includes the so-called "fly-over" part of the country.

One of the major flaws in republican thinking is that they like to show a sense of "fairness" in dealing with democrats, and that is a monumental mistake. The republicans don't have to "give" the democrats anything, because they will take whatever they want to the detriment of republicans and the American people. Therefore, it is unnecessary for the republicans to compromise on any part of the Trump Infrastructure Plan, because if they do, they do so to the disservice of the American public. We made the point earlier in this book about the incredulous inability of republicans, in general, to understand how to confront democrats, because before they do anything, they reach for a copy of the *Marquess of Queensberry Rules* and prepare to fight as a lady or gentleman, while they take a sucker punch from a radical democrat mob of street fighters.

Where Do We Go from Here?

This is a question of great import. It appears as long as the democrats continue to control the House, not to mention a *weakly* republican controlled Senate, much hangs in the balance. If the House should be returned to the republicans by at least a 50-seat majority, there is hope for two years; however, with the democrat voter fraud and other malevolent actions by these anti-Americans, that is a distant, sanguine plea of desire. However, the House is not the only matter of concern. What about the duplicitous republican controlled Senate? Put another way, if conservatives have to rely on people like Lindsey Graham, that's like handing someone on a sinking row boat an oar. There are so many F-Rs in the Senate, that in 2020 the Republican Party must not lose a single seat and pick up a minimum of two seats. More would be better, if they should be true conservatives; however, that is not likely. Thus far, I have not even discussed the presidency, because if we change to a mentally disturbed anti-American democrat, it's hard to imagine what will really happen to America. All of us conservatives have fought long and hard for what we achieved in 2016, and we cannot countenance losing everything for another experiment *on* America. We do not want to be a historical footnote on the dust bin of America. Our Founding Fathers left us this smorgasbord of a delicious and a beautiful largess of independence, liberty, and freedom, which we must not or cannot squander if we want America to remain America.

———

Endnotes

1   Duggan, Wayne (February 13, 2017) What Happened To All The 'Shovel-Ready' Infrastructure Projects From the 2009 Stimulus Bill? https://www.benzinga.com/General/education/17/02/9036944/what-happened-to-all-the-sh... DePillis, Lydia (February 12 2018) [CNN] Trump unveils infrastructure plan, https://money.cnn.com/2018/02/11/news/economy/trump-infrastructure-plan-details/index....

2   DePillis, Lydia (February 12 2018) [CNN] Trump unveils infrastructure plan, https://money.cnn.com/2018/02/11/news/economy/trump-infrastructure-plan-details/index....

3   Lucia, Bill (May 22, 2019) Route Fifty, https://www.routefifty.com/Infrastructure/2019/05/infrastructure-trump-democrats/157196/

4   History – https://www.history.com/topics/us-states-/interstate-highway-system

5   RT (April 2, 2015) Bad bridges: Federal date shows US Infrastructure crumbling, https://www.rt.com/usa/246041-deficient-bridges-usa-infrastructure/

6   Lange, Jason & Johnson, Katanga (January 30, 2018) Crumbling bridges? Fret no America, it's not that bad [Reuters] https://www.reuters.com/article/us-usa-trump-bridges-idUSKBNIFKOJO

7   Thomas, Lauren & Schoen, John (March 9, 2017) Engineers give America's infrastructure a near failing grade, [CNBC/politics] https://www.cnbc.com/2017/03/09/engineers-give-americas-infrastructure-a-near-failing-g...

8   Street, Chriss (March 18, 2019) Complete Failure at Oroville Dam, *American Thinker*, https://www.americanthinker.com/blog/2019/03/complete_failure-at_oroville_dam.html

9   Goodkind, Nicole (January 5, 2018) Trump Infrastructure Plan Includes Elon Musk – Style High-Speed Rail Tunnels And Eminent Domain, *Newsweek Magazine*, https//:www.newsweek.com/infrastructure-trump-elon-musk-high-speed-rail-hyperloop-77...

10 Ibid.

11 Shelbourne, Mallory (May 17, 2018) Trump's infrastructure plan hit dead end, *The Hill*, https://thehill.com/policy/transportation/388071-trumps-infrastructure-plan-hits-a-dead-end

12 Pramuk, Jacob (January 22, 2018) https://www.cnbc.com/2018/01/22/trump-news-infrastructure-plan-would-target-trumps-ru...

13 Laris, Michael (March 1, 2018) Trump wants to pass out billions for rural infrastructure. But what counts as "rural"? *Washington Post*, https://www.washingtonpost.com/local/trafficandcommuting/trump-wants-to-pass-out-billi...

Chapter 9

The Second Amendment
and Gun Control

Amendment II

*A well regulated Militia, being necessary to the
security of a free State, the right of the people to keep
and bear Arms, shall not be infringed.*

Over the past 50 or 60 years, the Second Amendment has become
one of the most controversial amendments of the Constitution. It is
also, interesting to note that only the First Amendment, regarding
free speech and expression, preceded the Second Amendment. It is
reasonable to assume that there was a priori in the compilation of
the initial amendments, especially the Bill of Rights. Since it was five
or ten decades ago when the Democrat Party was hijacked, either
interestingly or coincidentally, this is about when the left went into
high gear to undermine the basic principles of this republic. Efforts
to assail and assault the Second Amendment, thus far, have not been
nearly as successful as anti-America delusional democrats would
have preferred, but they are not discouraged. Every time a mass
shooting occurs, these leftists begin railing for some form of gun
control; however, the president has always stood with conservative
Americans in support of the Second Amendment and all of us expect
nothing less now.

Unfortunately, President Trump listens to his daughter, Ivanka,
and son-in-law, Jared, among other democrats, more than he should.
After the mass murders in Texas and Ohio in 2019, the president
wavered a bit on gun control measures and thinks that more
background checks will reduce mass killings in the U.S. Obviously,
he is misinformed and hasn't bought a gun recently, because it takes
at least three days to pass the normal background check before

you can actually gain possession of a handgun you have already purchased. I know that is true of Florida, Nevada, and Arizona; the other states have similar regulatory requirements. Apparently, gun-grabbers of the left want We the People disarmed in any way that it can be achieved.

There are hundreds of millions of guns in America, criminals will always be able to get a firearm at will; however, law-abiding citizens will be jerked around by government officials who have all the armed protection one can imagine. Thank God for the National Rifle Association (NRA) because that organization stands firmly in support of the Constitution and the Second Amendment. Reportedly, the NRA has an estimated five-million members.[1] Initially, my hope and prayer was President Trump would handle the awful mass murders delicately because if a significant percentage of voting members of the NRA just don't vote, this will make the president's reelection more difficult. Even worse, what about the massive number of avid gun owners who are not even members of the NRA? According to the Pew Center, approximately 30% of Americans own a gun.[2] What if even a small fraction of them also decided to just sit out the 2020 election? This is the danger of single-issue voting. Patriotic Americans do not like any intimation that the Second Amendment might be in jeopardy. I have heard President Trump state emphatically time and again at rallies, "Your Second Amendment is under siege." He might want to keep that in mind before he signs a democrat and F-R (fake republican) bill into law, because we know how both parties are prone to kneejerk reactions. My hope and prayer became a realization on August 15, 2019 at a rally of more than 11,000 in Manchester, New Hampshire SNHU arena with at least that many attendees outside, hoping to get into the arena where the president made his position on the Second Amendment abundantly clear. He made it unequivocal that he was and is a staunch supporter of the Second Amendment. I think the attendees at that raucous rally really needed to hear him address the issue head on, and he did, apparently to their satisfaction. In addition, on August 20, 2019, he reaffirmed to Wayne Lapiere of the NRA that he is not in favor of extended background checks.

Then, there was a crazed shooter in Philadelphia who apparently lost it. In that case, the fact is all the background checks and red flag laws which could have been conjured would not have prevented this particular gunman from shooting and wounding six police officers in that city on August 14, 2019. The perpetrator was a known criminal who was a convicted felon and had several guns/weapons which he was not supposed to have in his possession. It was nothing short of a minor miracle that none of the police officers were not killed. Philadelphia Police Commissioner, Richard Ross, Jr., told reporters, "We are very, very lucky with six police officers being shot in one incident . . . It is nothing short of astounding that . . . we didn't have more of a tragedy."[3] The fact is that the entire expanded background check argument and red flag laws are a spurious syllogistic exercise in futility.

Because I am not a single-issue voter and God willing, I will be voting for President Trump in 2020 and hope all thinking people will follow suit. He is the best thing that has happened to America in modern times, but I must voice some disappointment that he acquiesced to the voices of sinister leftists in this country on an issue which stands on solid constitutional grounds. In that regard, he has shown his imperfection and humanity, because he loves his family, as he should; even though, their advice has not always been sound. I know I heard his message loud and clear on gun laws at the Southern New Hampshire University arena. Hopefully, he heard the message of We the People as clearly as we heard his.

What is an "Assault Weapon"?

One thing is certain, delusional democrat's and the leftist media's drum beat of hyperbolic hysteria is incessant, unrelenting, and ignorant regarding so-called "assault weapons". Assault weapons and assault rifles have been conflated which is not accurate. Two respected professors, Bruce H. Kobayashi and Joseph E. Olson, writing in the Stanford Law and Policy Review, concluded, "Prior to 1989, the term "assault weapon" did not exist in the lexicon of firearms. It is a political term, developed by anti-gun publicists to expand the category of "assault rifles".[4] The operative word is political, because this is what the entire disingenuous argument is all about—either weakening the Second Amendment or eliminating it entirely. That would undermine America to the point that anti-Americans can undo America as we know it.

The Second Amendment is this nation's centurion. "Here's the point: 'assault weapons' is a made-up term that applies to whatever best serves democrats who are pushing gun control at any given time. After all, the *New York Times* reports that the term 'assault weapons' is a 'myth' democrat created in the 1990s."[5] Of course, it's a myth. Ignorant people make uninformed statements all the time. Much of what is said about "assault weapons" and "assault rifles" are because of cosmetics/appearance. If an AR-15 looks menacing like a typical military weapon, then it must be an "assault rifle".

Some unlearned people actually think [AR] stands for assault rifle. What it really stands for is the name of the company (Armalite Rifle) which developed it about 60 years ago.[6] As we have already established, the nomenclature "assault weapons" is a faux "technical" descriptor which has no basis in fact. Here *are* some facts. An AR-15 is a semi-automatic rifle, which means that the trigger must be pulled each time for a round to be expended. A loaded AR-15 weighs about 7.5 pounds. It is not a fully automatic rifle. It is not a machine gun. The law does not allow for American citizens to own, purchase, or use machine guns. It is the most popular rifle in America with approximately three-million sold. Wild game hunters really like this rifle, as well as citizens who have them primarily in their homes for self-protection.

Many years ago, when we resided in Laughlin, Nevada, I was target practicing with my handguns and shotgun when I encountered a young man from California who was in the possession of an AR-15. I watched him shoot for a while into the top of a mountain. He must have noticed my curiosity, because he soon suggested that I shoot his rifle. At first, I declined, because I was a little embarrassed that I had become so fixated upon him and his AR-15; however, after much urging by him, I did shoot his rifle a couple of times. I wasn't about to shoot anymore, because every round cost him a dollar! I must admit, I did really enjoy shooting it. Even back then, the AR-15 with a scope did cost around $2,000. Finally, just to reinforce the truth about so-called "assault weapons" it is important to note, "As used by the media, politicians, and gun control activists, "assault weapons" is a loosely defined term for a semiautomatic civilian firearm that has the **appearance**—but not the function—of a fully automatic military firearm."[7]

The left has been determined to prevent gunowners from having their weapon of choice for many decades. One way to attack the gun issue was by limiting the number of rounds a magazine could hold. This is incrementalism at its best. Just chip away in any manner possible. No matter what they do, they will fail, because America's patriots will never give up their guns. As an aside, for their edification, ten-round clips have not been the solution to preventing mass murderers from killing more innocent people. Killers just bring more loaded clips. Killer criminals will do whatever is necessary to carry out their evil deeds. That's one of the reasons law-abiding Americans need to bare arms. When the police might be minutes away, an armed citizen just might have only seconds to intervene in order to save lives. We are not a lawless society, and citizens must be able to defend themselves and others for the sake of our civilization. Yes, of course, we want the professionals to do this, but when they are not immediately available, it is incumbent upon American patriots to do that which is lawful and necessary to enforce the law.

Crucial Supreme Court Decisions

It was in 2008 that a man named Heller challenged the constitutionality of Washington, D.C., in that, it disallowed him from owning a handgun in a case of District of Columbia v. Heller (07-290).

In a 5-4 decision, the Court, meticulously detailing the history and tradition of the Second Amendment at the time of the Constitutional Convention, proclaimed that the Second Amendment established an individual right for U.S. citizens to possess firearms and struck down the D.C. handgun ban as violative of that right. . . . Further, the Court suggested that the United States Constitution would not disallow regulations prohibiting criminals and the mentally ill from firearm possession.[8]

It is instructive to note that the Court did suggest that regulations might be put in place which would prohibit the mentally ill and criminals from possessing a firearm. President Trump has made it clear, that when it comes to so-called "gun control", he is very concerned about the mentally ill having possession of or access to firearms. Based on the president's comments, any so-called gun "control" legislation will have to include/address the mental illness issue before he will sign it into law. Good common-sense dictates that if one of our citizens has documented and unequivocal mental stability issues, that person should never own or have access to a deadly weapon.

McDonald v. Chicago (o8-1521)

This Supreme Court case was petitioned by Otis McDonald on the heels of the District of Columbia v. Heller in which McDonald saw significant similarities. He argued that, "the right to bear arms is a fundamental right that states should not be able to infringe."[9] Of course, Chicago argued that it should be able to "tailor" firearm to local needs. "In a five-four split decision, the McDonald Court held that an individual's right to keep and bear arms is incorporated and applicable to the states through the 14th Amendment's Due Process Clause."[10] This Clause provides for the incorporation of the Bill of rights, substantive due process, procedural due process, and prohibition against vague laws. It essentially ensures that "no person is deprived of his life, liberty, or property without Due Process of law."[11]

A Stunning Stun Gun Decision

A homeless woman, Jaime Caetano, was arrested in 2011 for being in the possession of a stun gun. She claimed that a friend had given her the device because she feared an ex-boyfriend who was twice her size. When she was arrested, the authorities viewed this as related to the Second Amendment, in that, it had been categorized as a dangerous weapon. In Massachusetts, that was an unlawful carry. She was convicted, placed on probation, and then appealed, citing the McDonald and Heller cases. Over time, this case eventually was heard by the Supreme Court of the United States; wherein, SCOTUS vacated the Massachusetts Supreme Judicial Court (SJC) decision on stun guns.

Executive Director, Jim Wallace, of the Gun Owners Action League weighed in, "I think it's about time the Massachusetts court was told to respect the civil rights of gun owners. It's been pretty clear since the Heller and McDonald cases they were looking for any excuse to limit our Second Amendment rights."[12] It seems that Mr. Wallace is speaking the obvious because his point is well-taken. Massachusetts is a leftist state which follows any action it can to weaken the Second Amendment. In the Senate, it is led by democrats Ed (Green New Deal) Markey and Elizabeth (Faux Cherokee Indian) Warren—two rabid anti-Americans. All of the nine districts in Massachusetts are represented by democrats, including Ayanna Pressley—member of the "unmodsquad". It's as though a liberal virus is plaguing the citizens of the state of Massachusetts, which renders logic and reasoning impotent. Otherwise, it would seem that at least one republican would be serving in the Senate or the House. It must really roil these citizens that President Donald J. Trump crushed their candidate Hillary Rodham Clinton in 2016. When President Trump wins again in 2020, he will still be their president and ours until January of 2025!

Disarmed Citizens

The Founders of this great republic understood why an armed citizenry was imperative. At the time of the forming of this divine American experiment, people relied heavily upon their weapons to hunt animals so that they could help feed their families. A rifle, black powder, and ball were more important than frying pans, pots, plates, and bowls. The latter would be of little use without the former. In those times, the gun also had other overarching purposes. The Founders knew of the significance of self-defense and self-preservation. They were also keenly aware that any federal government formed would need to fear the citizens it was created to serve in the eventuality that the government should ever become tyrannical. In general, they were students of history and had read about or lived under despotic regimes which enslaved it citizens, disallowing the bells of freedom to ring across the land, and in this new world that was not about to happen. They had been subjects of King George III who was unreasonable, recalcitrant, and ignored their pleas. Throughout much of his life, he suffered episodic periods of insanity, and the loss of the colonies greatly exacerbated his condition. By the time he died, King George III was considered to be half-mad.[13]

What about Venezuela without guns?

The citizens of Venezuela discovered much to their chagrin what it is like to be without guns after . . . "President Hugo Chavez had his rubber stamp legislature pass the Control of Arms, Munitions and Disarmament Law. The public generally supported it at the time. The law stripped law-abiding Venezuelans of every firearm and round of ammunition they could legally own."[14] Before this occurred, the citizens had been enjoying the benefits of Bolivarian socialism. This is the socialist Bernie Sanders way into the extinction of individual freedom and liberty for America.

Venezuela was the envy of South America, because before its foray into the dark world of socialism, it was wealthy and the citizens were doing well. Today, they, the poor, are foraging for food in garbage cans and dumps, as rich socialists enjoy life as though most of the citizens, who are the poor, don't even exist. This is simply what does happen when someone decides to entirely ruin an economy. And that is what Bolivarian socialism has done, first under Chavez and now Maduro. This is not, as some try to say, about the declining oil price, that has affected other producers and hasn't led to the same sort of problems. These problems also started before the decline in the oil price. What did actually happen was a deliberate decision to destroy the price system.[15]

If anyone has doubts about the cause of Venezuela's economic collapse, just juxtapose capitalist Norway, which is highly dependent upon oil, to Venezuela. Despite the downward spiral of oil prices, the citizens of Norway are flourishing. This is what happens when socialism or any other economic system is in place. Only capitalism has lifted the poor from poverty to prosperity. Sadly, though most Venezuelans would like to oust Maduro, they don't even have guns/ weapons with which to resist this dictator. This serves as another reminder why we Americans will never give up our guns, regardless of left-wing lunatics like socialist Bernie Sanders and the entire delusional, radical Democrat Party. The Trump administration is in support of the people of Venezuela, but they have nothing with which to fight the despot Maduro. The gave up their guns.

<u>Historical Citizen Disarmament</u>

If we look back to the mid-1930s, we can see the early efforts to extinguish the Jewish people by Nazi Germany, because German Jews gave up their guns. The same is true of the poles and the Ukrainians. If people magically became sheep, they had better hope and pray they have a benevolent shepherd. Though Aristotle thought that a benevolent dictatorship is the best form of government, we still have not seen that occur in civilization. If truth be known, the Australians and citizens of Great Britain regret not being able to own the gun(s) of their choice legally, because crime is still a problem in both of those countries. The truth is, Australia's gun grabbing hasn't prevented mass murders. For instance, in Darwin, four men were killed and one woman was wounded by shotgun blasts. The perpetrator used a pump shotgun which was banned. "It was Australia's third <u>mass shooting</u> since the country introduced tough gun laws in response to a 1996 massacre in which a lone gunman armed with two semi-automatic assault rifles killed 35 people in Tasmania state."[16] This is just another kneejerk reaction of Australian elected officials, much like the gun grabbing delusional democrat lefties in the U.S.A.

What about gun-fearing citizens of Great Britain? Perhaps, gun control is not what it was all cracked up to be. The country, which has tightly restricted gun ownership since 1996, has seen double-digit rises in criminal activity across the board in 2017, including a 26 percent rise in knife crime (the highest since 2011), 27 percent rise in firearm crimes and 19 percent rise in overall violent crime. . . . According to the *The Telegraph*, latest figures confirm London is more dangerous than New York, noting that New York and London have similar populations (about 8 million), but in London burglary is six times more likely, rape is three times more likely, and the risk of being robbed is 50 percent higher.[17]

As an American citizen and one who loves England/the United Kingdom, I take no pride in writing about the travails of a tremendous nation. Personally, I have enjoyed visiting London and other parts of England. She is one of our strongest allies. Her people are good, sturdy citizens of lofty character. We have at least one of our great English friends still living in Middlesex, England. When I hear the music and song of God Save the Queen, I always think I should stand in honor of a great nation.

In summary, the United States is like no other country on Earth. This is an exceptional nation. We are guided by the Declaration of Independence, the Constitution, and the Bill of Rights, and those are the best arguments for us not trying to emulate other great countries and nations. No other nation has these brilliant, bedrock documents as a political sextant which guides us through murky, menacing, and treacherous waters. The intention of this book is about President Donald J. Trump and his support of the Second Amendment of the Constitution, and he has stated without equivocation that he is fully supportive of the aforementioned amendment. The Framers of our Constitution ensured that We the People would be able to defend ourselves from despots and tyrannical figures who might be able to temporarily dupe the citizenry long enough to turn them into subjects. If that should ever happen, We the People will be able to rise up and take back our nation because we are armed.

———

Endnotes

1   *Mother Jones Magazine* (March 7, 2018) The NRA Says It Has 5 Million Members. Its Magazines Tell Another Story. https://www.motherjones.com/politics/2018/03/nra-membership-magazine-numbers-1/ Pew Research Center (June 22, 2017) [*Social & Demographic Trends*] https://www.pewsocialtrends.org/2017/06/22/the-demographics-of-gun-Ownership/

2   Pew Research Center (June 22, 2017) [Social & Demographic Trends] https://www.pewsocialtrends.org/2017/06/22/the-demographics-of-gun-Ownership/

3   Holveck, Brandon, Kiggins, Steve & Lawrence, Elizabeth (August 15, 2019) Gunman surrenders after 'volatile' hourslong standoff in Philadelphia; 6 officers shot, *USA TODAY*, https://www.usatoday.com/story/news/nation/2019/08/14/Philadelphia-police-shooting-injured-standoff-...

4   The Truth About Assault Weapons, www.assaultweapon.info.

5   BREITBART (June 26, 2016), What is an Assault Weapon? https://www.breitbart.com/politics/2016/06/26/what-is-an-assault-weapon/

6   Lord, Debbie (August 3, 2019) [Cox Media Group National Content Desk] https://www.ajc.com/news/national/assault-weapon-assault-rifle-what-the difference/LPXLAj8zcHkPn2rLn3bOGK/

7   Assault Weapon Truth, The facts Buried Beneath the Rhetoric about "Assault Weapons", https://assaultweapontruth.com

8   Cornell Law School, Second Amendment, https://www.law.cornell.edu/wex/second_amendment

9   Cornell Law School (Oral argument: March 2, 2010) [McDonald v. Chicago (08-1521)] Second Amendment, Substantive Due Process, privileges and Immunities Clause, https://www.law.cornel.edu/supct/cert/08-1521

10 Rose, Veronica [Chief Analyst] (August 20, 2010) Summary of the Recent McDonald v. Chicago Gun Case, https://www.cga.ct.gov/2010/rpt/2010-R-0314.htm

11 Content Team [Legal Dictionary-Due Process] (January 22, 2015) Due Process, https://legaldictionary.net/due-process/

12 Quinn, Garrett (March 22, 2016) Supreme Court Vacates Massachusetts Supreme Judicial Court on Stun Guns, *Boston*, [News] https://www.bostonmagazine.com/news/2016/03/22/ supreme-court-vacates-stun-gun-ruling/

13 Pavao, Janelle, King George III, https://www.revolutionary-war. net/king-george-iii.html

14 Flamewarriors.net [Main Forum] (December 17, 2018) This Is What Happens to a Disarmed Populace, https:// www.flamerwarriors.net/forum/index.php?   thread/3761- this-is-what-happens-to-a-disa...

15 Worstall, Tim (June 21, 2017) Venezuela's Rich Aren't Suffering – That's Why Socialism's Such a Bad Idea, The Poor Do, *Forbes* [Opinion] https://www.forbes.com/sites/timworstall/2017/06/ 21/venezuelas-rich-arent-suffering-that

16 CBS/AP (June 4, 2019) At least 4 killed and "multiple crime scenes" after shooting in Australia, https://www.cbsnews.com/ darwin-australia-shooting-latest-updates-today-suspect-arr...

17 Burnett, David (October 27, 2017) Britain is Bleeding: Violent Crime Rises In England Despite Gun Control, [America's 1st Freedom] https://americas1stfreedom.org/articles/2017/10/27/ Britain-is-bleeding-violent-crime-...

Chapter 10

The Abortion Industry

Our country spiraled into a deep dark spiritual hole when the Supreme Court legislated from the bench in 1973 because its members saw something that was not in the 14th Amendment—the right to privacy. That landmark case is known as Roe v. Wade. Since that time, it has become a scourge upon our land. In 1969, Norma McCorvey (Jane Roe) of Dallas County Texas wanted to terminate her pregnancy. She was an impoverished young woman who already had two pregnancies which went to full term, resulting in two adoptions, and by the time this case had gotten to the Supreme Court, she had given birth and put a third child up for adoption as well. McCorvey challenged the anti-abortion law of Texas with the help of two female attorneys. In the Supreme Court, they went up against the district attorney of Dallas County—Henry Wade—who argued to uphold the Texas law, but the justices did not agree; hence, abortion upon demand became the law of the land.[1]

Since then, there have been well over 60,000,000 abortions in the USA, ". . . that have destroyed the lives of unborn children."[2] Put into perspective, that number is *twice* the population of the top 15 cites in America. Think of it, that includes the populations of *New York City, Los Angeles, Chicago, Houston, Phoenix, and 10 other large municipalities.* Try to imagine all of those cities without people. Because of abortions since 1973, the 15 cities mentioned only put us *half-way there!* We have no way of knowing but some of these helpless and vulnerable little people might have been the key to curing many of the diseases which plague those of us whom have had the opportunity to live. The 50th anniversary of this miscarriage of justice came in 2018 when the pro-life movement had their 45th March for Life. In case you missed it, President Trump spoke at that march in support of pro-life—not pro-death.

It is salient to note that a *taxpayer funded* organization—Planned Parenthood (PP)—has been responsible for the death of 7.6 million children of the total number cited above.[3]

This is the mantra of the Democrat Party—abort, abort, abort. The lives of these precious, tiny human beings were snuffed out in those clinics which trafficked in abortion. Worse, it is and was a common practice to dismember the babies while still in the womb. These merchants of death meticulously rip off arms, legs, and other parts of the baby's body with forceps as they harvest their parts which later are to be sold for profit. Does anyone really believe that these tiny people do not feel pain? We know for a fact that these babies feel and pain. There have been countless times when this has been scientifically demonstrated while still in the womb. It has been substantiated numerous times after about 20 weeks, pain is experienced by a "fetus." The word fetus is used here because it can also be called an "unviable tissue mass," which is a way of dehumanizing the killing of helpless humans. We have been so desensitized that many in our world cannot distinguish right from wrong. Essentially, they are intellectually, morally, and emotionally bankrupt. Many of our fellow Americans do not want to discuss or even think about the killing of a viable human being. I understand it completely, because it calls into question of what and who we have become. None of us want to entertain thoughts of barbarism, torture, and pain suffered by babies, but it's happening everyday all over this magnificent but numb country. Governor Ralph Northam of Virginia, who is a pediatric neurologist by profession, took abortion/ infanticide a step farther when he spoke about what happens to a baby outside the womb.

> *If a mother is in labor, I can tell you exactly what would happen. The infant would be delivered. The infant would be kept comfortable. The infant would be resuscitated if that's what the mother and the family desired, and then a discussion would ensue between the physicians and the mother, Northam said, alluding to the physician and mother discussing whether the born infant should live or die.*[4]

It has been said that physicians often try to play God. Is that what Dr. Northam and other physicians are doing? Is it his, the mother, and family's call to decide life or death of a living, breathing, helpless, and vulnerable human being? He speaks as though the "infant" is not a person. He could be talking about a puppy, kitten, or even an inanimate object, or a fruit like an apple or an orange. This is arrogance at a level that everyone would need pure oxygen just to sustain their own life. Could this all be accounted for because of a Narcissistic Personality Disorder (NPD) (God Complex)? NPD is characterized by . . . "the Diagnostic and Statistical Manual of Mental Disorders as a pervasive pattern of grandiosity, need for admiration, and a lack of empathy."[5] This is a generalized description of how many professionals and elected officials behave in this country when it comes to aborting a baby. The lack of empathy and human compassion is astounding. A primary coping mechanism is the nonacceptance of an embryo, fetus, or unviable tissue mass actually being a baby—life given by our Creator. The hard reality of abortion is brutal and unforgiving. As a result, people tend to avoid any discussion about this barbarism.

Margaret Sanger (1883-1966) – Founder of Planned Parenthood (PP)

This eugenicist also thought she could play God, as one who believed in cleansing the human population of undesirable groups of humanity. Obviously, only a person of such dubious character could be the founder of an organization to help with the purification of the human race. Let's look at some of her "endearing" words and comments.

- <u>Blacks, immigrants, and indigents</u>:
  . . . human weeds, reckless breeders, spawning human beings who never should have been born.
- <u>Sterilization and racial purification</u>:
  For the purpose of racial *purification* couples should be rewarded who chose sterilization.
- <u>Regarding the right of married couples to bear children</u>:
  Couples should have to submit an application to have a child.

- <u>The reason for birth control:</u>
  Is to create a race of thoroughbreds.
- <u>The handicapped and mentally ill</u>:
  Less from the unfit, and more from the fit—that is a primary purpose for birth control.
- The extermination of blacks: "We do not want word to go out that we want to exterminate the Negro population," she [Sanger] said.[6]

Regarding this last goal of Sanger and PP, it is being realized long after the death of Sanger in 1966. "Minority women constitute only about 13% of the female population (age 15-44) in the United States, but they underwent approximately 36% of the abortions. . . . According to the Alan Guttmacher Institute, black women are more than 5 times as likely as white women to have an abortion. . . . On average, 1,876 black babies are aborted every day in the United States."[7]

I cannot speak for everyone, but this is very disturbing and troubling. We are talking about the mass killing of black babies. Perhaps, that's one of the reasons PP has so many of its abortion "clinics" in, around, and near the black populace. As an American and human being, if this is not ungodly, then what is? How can responsible citizens/people stand idly by while these atrocities go unabated under the banner of a <u>woman's right to choose</u>. In the case of every abortion, each woman gave up her right to choose when she decided to commit an act which just might result in the creation of a human being. She gave up her "right to privacy" when she made the decision to have an unprotected sexual interlude. As a male, I understand the male libido. I also, comprehend the consequences of male irresponsibility and the cajoling of a woman into a sexual act which can have devastating consequences—pregnancy. As the old adage goes, it does take two to tango, but a potential dance partner doesn't have to agree to any kind of dance—the right to choose.

<u>Modern Planned Parenthood (PP)</u>

In July of 2019, the rabid and irrational leadership, the board, of Planned Parenthood (PP) actually fired CEO Leana Wen for refusing to say men can get pregnant. That is a ludicrous and an insane assertion. If it were possible for men to physically get pregnant, abortion would end overnight, because common sense tells me that a man does not have a womb; moreover, would the baby have to travel through his urethra before making its entry into the world? I think not, and some men have complained vigorously about the passing a kidney stone! Insofar as the leadership was concerned, Wen was not aggressive enough in her conviction to kill babies. She had not been on the job for even a year. "As reported by The Daily Wire on Tuesday, the country's largest abortion provider abruptly kicked President Leana Wen to the curb after just 10 months at the helm reportedly because Wen refused to say men can get pregnant and wasn't aggressive enough pushing the life-ending procedure." In some delusional way, they wanted transgender and other misguided cretins included in her vernacular.[8] Apparently, these mentally disturbed people do not understand basic fundamentals of biology. Whether or not they or anyone else likes it, there are only two scientifically identified genders—male and female—got it! If a person is not a female or a male, they don't exist, that is, people can believe whatever they wish about themselves but that does not change science or its reality. It is folly to believe that there are dozens of so-called genders. Based on what? Does it depend upon how an individual might feel today? This is new-age nonsense. We are what we are. Get used to it.

<u>The Evolution of Donald Trump</u>

President Trump has not always been pro-life, because there was a time when he was pro-death. The term pro-choice is a misnomer. There is no real choice for an unborn baby, because it is death. The term "pro-choice" is another way of saying "pro-abortion", but that sounds too harsh, sobering, and factual. As that great line from the movie *A Few Good Men* states, "You can't handle the truth!" As an aside, that was an adlib by Jack Nicholson. That famous sentence was not in the script. Originally, "pro-choice" was in Donald Trump's script regarding abortion. He like millions of Americans have evolved on this issue. As the populace has been educated on the barbarism thrust upon tiny human beings, change has occurred.

Knowledge is truly the sunshine which triumphs over the darkness of this inhumane practice. When people become aware of what really happens to these embryos, fetuses, and god forbid I should use the term babies, but that is what they are—tiny, helpless human beings who have no choice but the finality of their little lives. Many of them are ripped apart a piece at a time with the cold steel of forceps, wielded by a skilled physician who has deluded him or herself into believing that this is a job which must be done.

What specifically happened to Donald Trump? He often credits friends for his change of perspective, "What happened is friends of mine years ago were going to have a child, and it was going to be aborted. And it wasn't aborted. And that child today is a total superstar, a great, great child. And I saw that. And I saw other instances. And I am very, very proud to say I am pro-life."[9] Though the president is pro-life, he does make exceptions when it comes to rape, incest, and the life of the mother.[10] Despite that, President Trump loves children. He seems to have a truly "soft-spot" when it comes to the little ones.

Planned Parenthood (PP) Funding

At the heart of PP is money. It is a business which seeks to increase its income by whatever means. One of the revenue streams is the selling of baby parts, which is a rather lucrative venture. In 2016, Kelsey Bolar, senior writer and producer at The Daily Signal reported some very disturbing numbers regarding the dollar value of baby parts. This information was provided to a special republican House panel which was investigating this matter. For example, a fetal brain fetched $3,340; upper and lower limbs with hands and feet go for $890; skull matched to upper and lower limbs go for $595; human fetal tissue, 10 at $595 each equates to $5,950. There are other parts which also go for a hefty sum. It's not uncommon for a Planned Parenthood abortion clinic to turn an annual profit exceeding $40,000.[11]

Now, because of the Trump administration, new restrictions have caused Planned Parenthood to back away from Title X funding rather than comport with the guidelines. What's disgusting is, *this represents only four percent of its annual budget*! "Prior to its withdrawal, Planned Parenthood was receiving $60 million of the $286 million allocated annually through Title X. The organization will continue to receive roughly $500 million in annual Medicaid reimbursements from the federal government."[12] As an American taxpayer, I vociferously object to any of my taxes being spent on an organization like PP! I do not believe in killing unborn, innocent, and tiny human beings. Every American should be outraged about this. Even if you believe in abortion, you should object to spending tax dollars on this amoral provider of abortions. It is not a charitable organization doing good things for the general population. It is a nefarious business which has embraced Margaret Sanger's level of evil insanity.

PP doesn't like employees who blow the whistle on this organization which is bereft of decency and morality. Amy Johnson, a former PP director, now of the movie *Unplanned* fame, has been in the crosshairs of this abortion business for some time now. She's not alone, others have come forth with damning evidence about the "practices" of PP. For example, Mayra Rodriguez sued PP in October of 2017, because she claimed wrongful termination. She argued that at least one doctor was guilty of "high complication rates" in aborting babies. As a result, she was dismissed. Ironically, this illegal immigrant had worked for PP for 17 years and the adjudication of her case resulted in a jury decision of Arizona citizens who awarded her $3 million in damages in August of 2019.[13] Does anyone actually believe that PP did not know Rodriguez was an illegal immigrant during these 17 years? What does that say about our legal system? It awarded $3 million to an *illegal immigrant!* Apparently, some Arizonans don't have a clue about the enforcement of law. This woman should be detained by Arizona police and turned over to ICE officials for deportation to her home country. She has no business in America. It's good that this fraudulent organization just might have to pay out $3 million, but they just might choose to appeal this decision, and if they do, this could go on for some time. When it comes to jury awards, it seems nothing is ever really final. Never count a cent until the funds are in your bank account. Besides, Rodriquez is an illegal immigrant, that is, she is and has been in this country for a very long time.

The Name Planned Parenthood (PP)

It's curious, but even the name of Planned Parenthood is phony. This abortion clinic is not about parenthood in any real serious form. It's about "UNparenthood." The purpose of this business is to make sure that babies are not born—that a woman does not become a parent. It would seem that a descriptor more fitting is in order, but the truth, an appropriate moniker, would not be socially acceptable. There seems to be enough willing and able abortion doctors to help PP ensure that women don't have babies. For example, it was reported in mid-September 2019 that after an abortion doctor had passed away more than 2,000 fetal remains were found on Dr. Ulrich George Klopfer's property.[15] Can it be assumed that this is an anomaly? In reality there's no telling how much of this is going on in America. We've already seen the barbarism of Dr. Kermit Barron Gosnell who is serving three life sentences for killing babies.[16] At the time of his sentencing he was 72 years old, but why *three life sentences?!* Why should taxpayers provide him with food, housing, and medical care? A monster who snips, cuts, and twists the life out of babies should no longer be on this Earth. "Gosnell proudly displayed jars of severed babies' feet as trophies. . . . And if murdering babies born alive (by severing their spinal cords with scissors) wasn't enough, Gosnell, who is black, made sure that his white 'patients' were placed in the cleaner rooms while all the others were placed in the filthy rooms."[17] Where was the rage when this so-called "doctor" was practicing his craft? The sounds of rage and anger from the leftists have been deafening. Why wasn't Gosnell accused of being a racist for giving preference to white women over black? The hypocrisy of the democrat left is beyond words, it's nauseating. If the people for the ethical treatment of animals (PETA) had seen someone do this to little puppies or kittens, there would have been an outcry from California to New York. The nightly news would have story upon story about inhumane treatment of these helpless animals. Ironically, "inhumane" has the word "human" in it, but when it comes to tiny humans, inhumane doesn't seem to be applicable.

The Trump Administration's Conundrum

Abortion is a very difficult issue with which to deal, but it is a reality in America, and conservatives want it stopped. The president and his people will have to have at least two more true conservative patriots on the Supreme Court before Roe v. Wade can ever be successfully challenged. Some may say that there are enough conservatives on the Court to get it done now, but that is not a lead-pipe cinch. To illustrate, the 1973 Supreme Court was comprised of more republican presidential appointees than democrat. Nixon appointed four and Eisenhower appointed two which resulted in a 7-2 decision in Roe v. Wade.[14] In today's Court, Justices Thomas, Alito, and Gorsuch would more than likely be interested in correcting this Court injustice of long ago, but who knows about Kavanaugh and Roberts. There is no doubt that Sotomayor, Kagen, Breyer, and Ginsberg would not be supportive at all, which brings us to the next chapter (11) regarding the Supreme Court and Other Federal Judges.

———

Endnotes

1   HISTORY.COM EDITORS (Updated: May 15, 2019) Roe v. Wade, http://www.history.com/topics/topics/womens-rights/roe-v-wade

2   Ertelt, Steven (January 18, 2018) 60,069,971 Abortions in America Since Roe v. Wade in 1973 [LifeNews.com] https://www.lifenews.com/2018/01/18/60069971-abortions-in-america-since-roe-v-wade-i...

3   Yoder, Katie (March 7, 2018) Planned Parenthood has killed 7.6 million children since 1973 [Live Action] https://www.liveaction.org/news/planned-parenthood-7 million-abortions-roe/

4   Kugle, Andrew (January 30, 2019) Northam on Abortion Bill: Infant Could Be Delivered and Then Physicians and the Mother Could Decide If It lives [The Washington Free Beacon] https://freebeacon.com/issues/northam-on-40-week-abortion-bill-infant-would-be-deliver...

5   The Wallstreet Psychologist (May 3, 2013) Narcissistic Personality Disorder (God Complex, http://www.thewallstreetpsychologist.com/recent_posts/narcissistic-personality-disorder-g...

6   Dew, Diane S. (copyright © 2001) Margaret Sanger, Founder of Planned Parenthood – In Her Own Words, http://www.dianedew.com/sanger.htm

7   Black Genocide.org, Abortion and the Black Community, http://www.blackGenocide.org/black.html

8   Ashley (Kimber) (July 17, 2019) Planned Parenthood Just Fired New CEO For Not Saying Men Can Get Pregnant [chicksontheright.com] https://www.chicksontheright.com/blog/2019/07/17/planned-parenthood-justfired-new-ceo-f...

9   Durkee, Alison (January 30, 2017) Protect Abortion Access, https://www.mic.com/articles/167090/wasn-t-trump-once-pro-choice-here-s-the-president-...

10 Ibid.

11 Bolar, Kelsey (April 20, 2016) In the Market for Fetal Body Parts, a Baby's Brain sells for $3,340 [The Daily

Signal] https://www.daily signal.com/2016/04/20/in-the-market-for-fetal-body-parts-a-babys-brain-...

12 Crowe, Jack (August 19, 2019) Planned Parenthood Refuses Title X Funding in Response to Trump Administration Restrictions [National Review] https://www.nationalreview.com/news/planned-parenthood-refuses-title-x-funding-in-response-to-trump-admins-restricts/

13 Parke, Caleb (August 19) Planned Parenthood whistle blower gets $3M from Arizona Court after wrongful termination [Fox News] https://www.foxnews.com/us/planned-parenthood-arizona-court-wrongful-termination

14 Schneider, Mercedes (updated November 9, 2016) [Contributor] *Huffington Post*,https://www.huffpost.com/entry/trump-supporters-roe-v-wade-was-decided-by-a-republic...

15 Olohan, Mary Margaret (September 14, 2019) Over 2,000 Fetal Remains Found On Late Abortion Doctor's Property, Sheriff's Office Says, [Daily Caller] https://Dailycaller.com/2019/09/14/thousands-fetal-remains-abortionist/

16 Bomberger, Ryan (Chief Creative Officer of The Radiance Foundation) [Too Many Aborted.com] www.toomanyaborted.com/Gosnell/

17 Lattanzio, Vince (May 15, 2013) Gosnell Sentenced to 3 Life Terms, Jurors Open Up, https://www.nbcphiladelphia.com/news/local/Gosnell-Sentenced-on-Other-Crimes-207525...

Chapter 11

Supreme Court and Other Federal Judges

It can hardly be argued that over the past several decades that an incredible liberalization of the federal court system has occurred. Even when supposed to be conservative presidents have made the appointments, surprisingly, they have "misjudged" the appointee with frequency, as mentioned in the previous chapter. It is often said that judges should not be conservative or liberal, that they be impartial in meting out justice. It would really be refreshing if that were the case, but that can only happen in a perfect world, and that is not a place in which we reside. Everything is now politicized to the point of absurdity—even Hurricane Dorian on Labor Day 2019. We have lower court federal judges mostly from the ninth circuit and other federal judges frequently stopping presidential actions all because they are delusional, obtuse liberals who dislike and reject just about everything President Trump proposes. These particular judges are beyond pathetic; they are incompetent and should be removed from the bench. Having said that, impeachment is a laborious and painful process, one not to be taken lightly and actually should be used more often.

For the most part, these radical, delusional judges are blinded by rabid hatred for President Trump and their personal desire to advance liberalism and socialism at all costs. These are the kind of federal judges who have no business piously sitting in a black robe while obfuscating the work of a duly elected president of the United States. In the majority of cases, these self-righteous, sanctimonious democrat judges were appointed by Barack Hussein Obama who has set this country back, culturally, morally and ethically in terms which are incalculable. The question arises is there a remedy for this reckless and irresponsible behavior? Yes, there is a corrective measure, but it is not an easy one, and it's called impeachment. "The Constitution requires that a judge can be removed by two steps.

A judge must first be impeached by majority vote of the House of Representatives and then convicted by a two-thirds vote of the Senate."[1] This is a tall order, because our government has become so corrupt and incorrigible that it has definitive characteristics of a banana republic. The elected officials, men and women, who sit in judgment of the citizens of the USA are so compromised that they have become politically paralyzed. To illustrate, right now in Congress, we have several congresspersons who should be expelled from that body for their anti-American and anti-Semitic statements and actions, but nothing will be done about it, because so many members of Congress have their own moral and ethical breaches and dilemmas which must remain hidden. They can be likened to the scribes and Pharisees who were challenged by Jesus in the 8th Chapter of John in the *Bible* to "cast the first stone." They [scribes and Pharisees] had brought an adulterous woman before him because the Law of Moses had required that she be stoned to death, but later when Jesus confronted her about the whereabouts of her accusers, she said that no one was any longer there who had condemned her, and Jesus commanded her to, "Go, and sin no more."[2] If these corrupt politicians would do as Jesus said, they would be forgiven as well, but sadly that will probably not happen because the Democrat Party appears to be godless in their actions and deeds, as well as a lot of fake republicans. Over the past several years, the democrats have attempted to remove God and prayer from the House of Representatives. They do not want anything to remind them that there will be an accounting when we all stand before God.

We have delineated, constitutionally, a way in which errant, rogue, and rascally judges can be removed from office, but that is not likely to happen; although, there is at least one situation in the recent past in which a federal judge has committed such egregious crimes that he was impeached and removed from the bench. Judge Alcee Hastings, a 1979 Carter appointee, was impeached for bribery in the amount of $150,000. When President Carter appointed him, he became Florida's first African-American federal judge. He had a co-conspirator who was convicted of the crime, but Hastings was acquitted and returned to the bench. This did not sit well with a special committee of the Eleventh Circuit Court of Appeals, and it concluded that Hastings was guilty and the panel recommended that he be impeached and removed from office. Ultimately, the House did its own investigative work and approved 17 articles of impeachment which put the ball in the "court" of the Senate which resulted in his removal from office on October 20, 1989. However, the weasels in the Senate did not vote to disqualify him from holding a future public office. As a result of that spineless act of omission, democrat Hastings was elected to the Congress in 1993 and has been there since that time.[3] My guess is he will remain in Congress until he draws his last breath. Here's the most important point. It's not Hastings as much as it is his constituency. What kind of people are they? Why would they continue to elect a person of such questionable character? This type of nonsense must be stopped. District 20 of Florida will have an opportunity to correct their mistake and elect a person of good behavior and character in 2020. That being said, it could be that the voters actually have little say in who's elected. South Florida is rife with democrat voter fraud, let's see if they are able to do the right thing.

Historical Impeachments

The Constitution was ratified in 1789, and according to the Federal Judicial Center, only fifteen federal judges have been impeached.[4] Over the past 33 years, <u>five of the total of fifteen federal judges</u> earned that fate. It should be noted that there are nearly 1,000 lifetime appointed federal judges. It's also interesting to note that only 10 federal judges were impeached before 1986—197 years!

- Harry E. Claiborne-U.S. District Court for the District of Nevada was impeached July 22, 1986 and was removed by the U.S. Senate, October 9, 1986.
- Alcee L. Hastings – U.S. District Court for the Southern District of Florida was impeached by the U.S. House August 3, 1988 and removed from office by the U.S. Senate October 20, 1989. As mentioned above, in 1993 he was elected to Congress.
- Walter L. Nixon – U.S. District Court for the Southern District of Mississippi was impeached May 10, 1989 by

the U.S. House and removed from office by the U.S. Senate November 3, 1989.

- Samuel B. Kent – U.S. District Court for the Southern District of Texas was impeached by the U.S. House June 19, 2009 and later resigned. On July 22, 2009 the U.S. Senate, sitting as a court of impeachment, dismissed the articles of impeachment.

- G. Thomas Proteous, Jr. – U.S. District Court for the Eastern District of Louisiana was impeached by the U.S. House March 11, 2010 and removed from office by the U.S. Senate December 8, 2010.

Though the impeachment process is difficult, there are times when that is the best alternative to move forward. "Decisions made by sitting Supreme Court justices are often felt throughout the country for decades, and sometimes even beyond. Not only does this add an incredible amount of gravity to the position, it makes the potential removal process quite the lengthy proposition."[5] In some ways, impeachment is a sad but necessary way to remove an undesirable.

It is obvious that there needs to be some significant changes made in regard to the U.S. judicial system. America has changed dramatically since the ratification of the Constitution, and the Founders left us the tool to change the Constitution to fit the needs of the nation in the ebb, flow, and currents of time. We understand why they gave lifetime appointments to federal judges, but should that practice be continued? Article III of the Constitution is the foundational component of our guiding document which delineates the duties of the Supreme Court and inferior federal courts. Alexander Hamilton (Publius) authored The Federalist Papers: No. 78 which gives us some insight into the intentions of the judiciary as related in Article III[6]. The requisite condition upon which a judge remains in office is based on "good Behaviour", intimating that there is no limit to their term of service. As an aside, Alexander Hamilton was 21 at the founding of this great republic. He was younger then than my current, youngest graduate student by about five years!

Age and Fitness Issues

In order to realize some perspective of the Founders, it is instructive to examine the issue of age as related to the times in which they founded this republic. As mentioned above, the youngest member of the Founding Fathers was Alexander Hamilton at 21 and the oldest was Benjamin Franklin at 70. The average age of this august body was 43.8, and John Adams was 41.[7] Keeping this in mind, during the liberty era of 1750-1800, life expectancy of the populace was only 36 years of age.[8] At age 70, they must have thought of Benjamin Franklin as Methuselah who lived to be 969.

In relative terms, let's examine the average age of the current makeup of the U.S. Supreme court, which by 2020 is 68. Ruth Bader Ginsburg will be 87 and Stephen Breyer will be 82, Clarence Thomas 72, Samuel Alito 70, and then we have the youngsters, Sonia Sotomayer at 66, John Roberts 65, Elena Kagan 60, Brett Kavanaugh 55, and the kid, Neil Gorsuch at 53.[9] Purely speculative of course, but it seems that the Founders would have been astonished to see citizens of this republic living to about 80 years of age. It's actually more than an age issue. What about fitness to serve? Personally, I recall watching William O. Douglas on television as he was being wheeled into the Court because of a massive stroke. "Then on the last day of 1974, while on vacation in the Bahamas, he suffered a massive stroke that left him permanently impaired. Confined to a wheelchair, his mental energy drained, Douglas struggled to continue his work on the Court, but could not do so."[10] That is the point. He could not do so. We have a similar situation now with Justice Ginsburg. Though philosophically we are at opposite ends of the spectrum, it gives me no great joy to conclude that she is unfit to continue to serve. She has and has had many serious health issues. I'm still puzzled by her working on the Court while in the hospital. Often, it's difficult to tell if she's napping, under the influence, or just resting her eyes. Though I do know, according to her, "In the old days, she says, now retired Justice David Souter would sit next to me and give her a jolt when she needed one. But Kennedy and Breyer are sort of timid about that."[11] She even admitted that she was not 100% sober at the State of the Union which Barack Obama gave in February of 2015.

In the history of our country it has not been uncommon for Supreme Court Justices to serve two or three decades on the Court, and in a few instances even more—not to mention other federal judges who are still serving well into their nineties. From a logical perspective, it would seem that at some point age and fitness does become a factor. The time has come for a reconsideration of lifetime appointments—demurring to "good Behaviour" as being the sole arbiter of fitness to serve. As mentioned earlier, we do have a constitutional tool which we can use to make course corrections going forth in the history of our judiciary. Even the concept of lifetime appointment, in these times, no longer seems valid or reasonable. Practically, every part of our government has become politicized, polarized, and damaged, and the judiciary has not been immune. The composition of the Court is democrat or republican, liberal or conservative. Their political views are manifested and usually in concert with the two-party system. The Constitution is almost an afterthought when it comes time for a liberal to cast a vote on the Court.

Just to make it clear, the Founders considered that the Supreme Court would be the weakest link of the three branches of government. It was to oversee, to ensure, that the other branches were acting in good faith and deed, and in the best interest of the citizens of America through a checks and balance perspective. In today's business terms, it was the HR Department for the nation. Metaphorically, the judiciary should be unbiased umpires. Using a baseball analogy, they were to objectively determine when the game was to start—call strikes, balls, time outs, outs, and when to stop the game; however, in my lifetime that has not been the situation. Contrary to the intentions of the Founders, the Court has become a rival of the Executive Branch as well as the Legislative Branch. The Court of today legislates from the bench. The Court is governed by a Freudian Super-ego, which flexes its muscles by attempting to be the conscience of America which is somehow on a lofty plain of morality and ethics high above all others. In the eyes of the Court, it is the final word on everything. It is in charge. It decides whether or not any actions taken or even contemplated comports with its super-ego ideals.

The Supreme Court is expected to render sound decisions for the nation based on the Constitution as written, not by what they wish or would like for it to have said. Simply stated, the Constitution is to be interpreted, not séanced. In actuality, there are limitations placed upon the Court despite its delusional, celestial view of itself. There are significant checks and balances which limits the judicial branch. For example:

- The Senate approves federal judges.
- The House of Representative can impeach federal judges and the Senate tries them.
- Congress has the power to initiate Constitutional amendments, establish inferior federal courts, and set the jurisdiction of courts.
- Federal judges are appointed by the executive branch.[12]

<u>Impeachment Abuse</u>

Though there are times when impeachment is a remedy but seldom used, we also must approach this with due diligence and caution, because judicial impeachment should not be used as a punishment for the rulings judges make. When judges are deciding cases based on their understanding of the facts, they should not have to concern themselves with powerful political forces who might disagree with their decision.[13] Historically, we know that there have been abuses of the power of impeachment. To illustrate, "In the heat of the 1996 presidential campaign, for example, both candidates—President Clinton and Senator Dole—attacked a sitting federal district court judge for ruling evidence inadmissible in a case against a drug courier and indicated they would support the judge's removal."[14] This kind of behavior is inappropriate to say the least and this is certainly not the only instance in which this has occurred.

At some point, most of us have vociferously disagreed with a decision of a judge, but we don't usually have the same set of facts before us as that judge. Mostly, when I disagree with a federal judge's ruling, it is one which is rendered from a radical democrat stronghold such as the ninth circuit, because it's not usually about what's right or the law, it's about trying to prevent President Trump from doing his job for the American people and thrusting forth liberalism and socialism. Nearly from the beginning, the president has been plagued by federal lower court interventions in his efforts to make America great again. The time has come for serious consideration being given to the limiting of the term a federal judge can serve on the court. Lifetime appointments are no longer applicable today. As has been discussed, we are living longer and the concept of "good Behaviour" is not as relative today as it was 200 years ago. It will take a constitutional amendment to change this, but that is why our Founders provided for the amendment process. As a people, we need to objectively examine the potential consequences of judicial term limits.

The Ending of Lifetime Tenures

Alexander Hamilton, as according to Federalist No. 78, was quite supportive of lifetime tenures. He also stated that the judiciary would be the least dangerous politically,[15] but we have an abundance of evidence today which contradicts that thinking. Most Americans have watched the president's efforts thwarted over the past nearly three years, time and again, by partisan politics led by liberalist and socialistic thinking and actions, which have temporarily blocked what the American people wanted and needed. Once again, regarding Hamilton's thinking:

> *There are, however, a couple of points that should be noted here. First is that Hamilton had supported, just the year earlier, lifetime tenures for both senators and the president—which he termed "[t]he supreme Executive authority of the United States to be vested in a Governour" before the name "president" had been decided. It is clear that Hamilton had a bias towards lifetime appointments for the most powerful offices.[16]*

This thinking is part of our problem today. The "supreme Executive authority", especially at the Senate level, thinks more highly of itself than it should. The voters of the United States hire/ elect these people to serve us, not the other way around. There is no senator or president, for that matter greater, than any citizen of the country. They work for We the People. They have been elected to serve us. Semantically, this is part of the problem with the term *Supreme* Court. It, too, thinks more highly of itself than it ought. The term "supreme" tends to lift a person to a high perch above all of the rest of us. A better term for the "Supreme Court" would be the "Senior Court" which means that it has seniority over all other courts. It is the final word on matters of law.

Regarding the Supreme Court, these nine judges have lifetime appointments. It is understandable why the Founders of that time granted this tenure. They wanted to ensure independence so that their decisions would not be compromised. It was vital that the politically powerful and influential would not be able to pressure these justices, but that was then, this is now. What we have today is a highly politicized Supreme Court which needs to be restrained. One of the best ways to do that is to limit its tenure, that is, term limit the members of the Supreme Court. Jason Gay has suggested that a term of 10 years[17] would be a reasonable tenure, which makes sense. From an implementation perspective, the terms of these judges could be staggered on a two-year basis or other time schedule. As mentioned earlier, to change the tenure of Supreme Court justices and other federal judges would require a constitutional amendment. That would take about 5-10 years if zealously pursued by a fervent bi-partisan number of politicians in the House and Senate, and at this point in time, a bi-partisan anything is delusional because of F-Rs and radical socialist democrats.

Trump Appointments

President Trump set a record in his first 200 days by appointing more judges than Presidents Obama, Bush, and Clinton."[18] To date, the most significant appointments have been to the Supreme Court— Neil Gorsuch and Brett Kavanaugh. The conservative credentials of Gorsuch, with one exception,[19] [not a precedent setting decision] are without question, but Kavanaugh's conservative bent is still to be determined. Judge Kavanaugh replaced the retired Supreme Court Justice Anthony Kennedy who was a so-called "swing vote" of sorts. In other words, he often voted with the liberals on the Court, which defies logic. In addition, Kavanaugh once clerked for Justice Kennedy. Interestingly, all of the law clerks he has hired are female, and according to Professor Chua of the Yale Law School, "For the more than 10 years I've known him, Judge Kavanaugh's first and only litmus test in hiring has been excellence. He hires only the most qualified clerks, and they have been diverse as well as exceptionally talented and capable."[20] Should we assume then that there were no highly qualified, exceptional male students he could have hired? I find that somewhat unrealistic and enigmatic. To me, the hiring of an all-female clerk of the Court staff is indicative of liberal thinking and action; although, as reported in *The Guardian*, they looked more like models.[21] At this point, the "jury" is still out on Justice Brett Kavanaugh. To coin a popular phrase of the president, "We'll see." It's interesting to note that the delusional Democrat Party is promising to impeach Kavanaugh if they take the White House and retain control of the House. Collectively, these people must be deranged.

If the president is to continue to nominate and get Senate approval for judges, the Republican party must not lose its grip in the Senate. If the Democrat Party finds a way to steal enough Senate seats in 2020, that will be devasting and paralyzing to the country. That is an essential reason for the GOP to do everything it can to not only hold on to the majority but to increase the number if at all possible, because the party is filled with F-Rs (fake republicans). It is without doubt that the Senate is being targeted and in jeopardy, and the Democrat Party is ruthless, unprincipled, and willing to do whatever it takes to stop the president from confirming judges. Nothing would make The Donkey Party more pleased than to neuter the president, and the key to doing that is by stopping the progress he has made in moving the judiciary more to the right of center where most Americans are philosophically and politically positioned. Despite their efforts to impede the progress of the president without [their] democrat support, he still has prevailed. This reinforces President Trump's resiliency and determination. This just underscores his intensity and propensity to keep on winning, winning, winning. Chapter 12 which follows asks a conspicuous question—where does America go from here?

———

Endnotes

1   Johan, James J. (February 19, 2018) Time to remove federal judges from office? [American Thinker] https://www.americanthinker.com/blog/2018/02/time_to_remove_federal_judges_from_of...

2   King James version of the *Bible*, John, CHAPTER 8.

3   Constitutional Law Reporter, https://constitutionallawreporter.com/2017/06/13/alcee-hastings-impeachment/

4   Staff, *The Tennessee Star* (February 11, 2017) Fifteen Federal Judges Have Been Impeached by the House of Representatives, https://tennesseestar.com/2017/02/11/fifteen-federal-judges-have-been-impeached-by-the-...

5   Ketchum, Dan (Match 29, 2019) Rules of Removing a Supreme Court Justice [Legal Beagle] https://legalbeagle.com/6596992-rules-removing-supreme-court-justice.html

6   Yale Law School [The Avalon Project] The Federalist Papers: No. 78, https://avalon.law.yale.edu/18th_century/fed78.asp

7   https://www.answers.com/Q/What_was_the_average_age_of_the_founding_fathers

8   http://www.legacy.com/life-and-death/the-death-liberty-era.html

9   GodVoter.org, Ages of Supreme Court Justices, https://www.godvoter.org/ages-of-supreme-court-justices, html

10 Oldman, Kit (November 11, 2004) Douglas, William O. (1898-198Richard0) https://www.historylink.org

11 Wolf, Richard (February 3, 2015) Justice Ginsburg: Not '100% sober' at State of the Union, *USA TODAY*, https://usatoday.com/story/news/politics/2015/02/13/supreme-court-ginsburg-state-of-the-union/23...

12 Lorcher, Trent – What are the powers of the Judicial Branch of Government? Article 3 of the U.S. Constitution Explained [Bright Hub Education] https://www.brighthubeducation.com/history-homework-help/56250-powers-granted-to-th...

13 Keith, Douglas (March 23, 2018) Impeachment and Removal of Judges: An Explainer, [Brennan Center.org]

https://www.brennancenter.org/blog/impeachment-and-removal-judges-explainer

14 Ibid

15 Gay, Jason C. (March 13, 2015) End Lifetime Judicial Appointments [The Federalist] https://the federalist.com/2015/03/13/end-lifetime-judicial-Appointments/

16 Ibid

17 Ibid

18 Lucas, Fred (August 10, 2017) Trump Appoints More Judges in 200 Days Than Obama, Bush, Clinton [Daily Signal] https://www.dailysignal.com/2017/08/10/Trump-appoints-more-judges-in-200-days-than-o...

19 Bleau, Hannah (April 17, 2018) Neil Gorsuch's latest Vote Surprises Conservatives And Liberals Alike...[Chicks On The Right!] https://www.chicksonright.com/blog/2018/04/17/neil-gorsuchs-latest-vote-surprises-conserv...

20 Kirchgaessner, Stephanie & Glenza, Jessica (September 20, 2018) 'No accident' Brett Kavanaugh's female law clerks 'looked like models', Yale professor told students [The Guardian] https://www.theguardian.com/us-news/2018/sep/20/Bret-kavanaugh-supreme-court-yale-am...

21 Ibid.

Chapter 12

Where Does America Go from Here?

Where does America want to go? There is a clear choice in 2020. The nation has reached a logical and undeniable *decision point*. The citizens of America can relitigate the past and wallow in an Obama world of depravity, foolishness, nothingness and try failed socialism or remain on a path to prosperity. The answer seems simple—the path to prosperity of course, but the delusional and socialist democrats have muddied the waters to the point many Millennials are actually considering rejecting our capitalist market system of economics for socialism—free everything! This "thinking" is not only flawed and folly, it is absurd and insane! With that said, the youth of our country are not entirely responsible for their fuzzy understanding of how the world works. They have been indoctrinated by liberal leftist teachers from K-12 in which civics and American history is no longer taught. Afterward, they have been dumped into colleges and universities into the waiting, eager hands of misguided professors all across this country who continue the leftist-communist brainwashing drumbeat with an intense fervor. Our so-called *institutions of higher learning* should be renamed according to what they have become—*institutions of higher propaganda*.

When university presidents, administrators, and professors disallow conservative voices to speak on their campuses, they are the ones who are intolerant, biased, and bigoted. From the time I was a freshman in college, I was able to express my opinion on issues which mattered to me, but even back in the 1960s and 1970s, I found myself in the crosshairs of liberal professors with an agenda who I reluctantly had to outmaneuver in order to pass a class. Unlike the Millennials of today, I had already been schooled in hard knocks. Most of these young people refuse a cup of coffee if it's not from Starbucks, and young people of my time were happy to just *get* a cup of coffee. The point which needs to be made is this is more than generational differences. It is about life choices, and the choice to be made in 2020 is pivotal to the survival of the United States of America.

Most of the Founders of this republic have been deceased for more than 200 years; yet, I hear their voices of warning about being able to keep this nation as they left it while it was still in its infancy. It is imperative that the road of prosperity not be littered with the putrid corpses of rotting socialism. The Bernie Sanders of the world, *unlike him*, are oppressed, starving, desperate for food and freedom; yet, he wants liberty loving Americans to surrender to an all-powerful burgeoning federal government. People like him need to go to a country of their choice which operates under the dictates of socialism or communism. I wonder why he didn't stay in the old communist Soviet Union when he and his wife honeymooned near Moscow decades ago. "In 1988, during the final years of the Cold War, Bernie and Jane Sanders spent their first days as newlyweds in the city of Yaroslavl, 160 miles northeast of Moscow . . . at the time of Sanders's honeymoon "'gulags still functioned'" and political prisoners were still "'being tortured in psychiatric 'hospitals'" . . . . Sanders is a wealthy commie who's never been keen on foreign policy."[1] Actually, he's never been especially keen on economic matters or systems of any kind as well. The man has been jobless most of his life and on the government dole. He doesn't understand work and the need to earn an honest living for a family. Simply stated, he doesn't have a clue.

Is America a Country of Laws or Outlaws?

Many in America, today, see two "justice" systems. Those privileged and powerful in this society are not concerned about the law or a justice system because they are immune to the laws, regulations, and rules which provide for civilization. They are essentially outlaws. Should there be any doubt about this claim, what about Bill and Hillary Clinton, James Comey, John Brennan, James Clapper, Peter Strok, Andrew McCabe and many others? They have been placed into a special category, unlike more than 99% of the citizens of America. Many people like myself have become disappointed, disturbed, and mystified by the powerful, the connected who break the laws with impunity and suffer no consequences. One thing is for certain, if there are no consequences for bad behavior, there will be no change.

<u>A Department of Justice (DOJ) Theorem</u>

There are differing metaphors and analogies which can be used to describe the inertia within the Justice Department. The Attorney General, William Barr, can be likened to the Dutch Boy, although Barr is more likely of Scottish or Irish lineage, who held *his finger in the dyke* until an adult arrived to help secure the dam because many were going to be swept away if the Dutch boy removed his finger. Wonder when the adult will arrive. Another plausible analogy is the *house of cards* metaphor. This is all about carefully balancing each card one against another because the removal of a single card will cause the entire house to crash to the ground. Regardless of which scenario you choose, it has been well-established that the DOJ is a house of impropriety of questionable behaviors, as well as the compromised Federal Bureau of Investigation (FBI) and others who have been involved in an, unprecedented in American history, attempted soft coup d'état against the president of the United States.[2] President Trump has been a target of both of these agencies even before he was overwhelmingly elected in 2016, and in this regard, according to news reports, fired former Deputy Attorney General Andrew (Andy) McCabe might get indicted. Will he be the sacrificial lamb? As an aside, if this is a "house of cards", the DOJ will have to work some incredible slight of hand for the entire house to remain standing. It is highly probable that at least two of the cards will never go down. At this point, only two agencies have been mentioned but there is evidence that the Central Intelligence Agency (CIA) was at least knee-deep, in this conspiracy, and others who coordinated the efforts of the failed coup from around the world.

> "Former CIA Officer and whistleblower Kevin Shipp says the attempted coup on Trump was a global conspiracy. Shipp explains, "'Yes this is a coup. This is the most shocking violation of the Constitution and criminal activity in the history, not just America, but of a western government.'"[3]

A point of caution, when the term *conspiracy* is used, the guilty insist that statements and accusations of that nature are all untrue, made-up fake stories which have no basis in fact. That claim is also true of the word *rumor* but with a rumor there is usually a nugget of truth buried within. Businesses and organizations use this as a tool on the in-house "grapevine" to prepare the employees for what is about to come. You may be assured that there is a lot more to a conspiracy than a "nugget" of truth. In the case of President Trump, we know of a number of other countries around the world who played a part in this coup. For example, it has been established that Italy[4] and England[5] were involved. Later in this chapter, there will be other discussion about the principalities and powers around the world interested in neutering President Trump and why. President Andrew Jackson in the 1820s-1830s had his battles with the banking industry which was controlled by foreign investors much like the Federal Reserve of the U.S. is today, and it's fair to say that Trump is not a fan of our private bank either.

While attempts abroad were underway to "correct" the 2016 presidential outcome, President Trump's detractors at home were feverishly and tenaciously doing all within their power to oppose and challenge him on every initiative he put forth. The entire democrat machine, leftist main stream media, liberal federal court system, and a significant cadre of fake republicans railed against him mightily, but they failed to subdue him. His political will reminds me of Jim Brown the great running back of the Cleveland Browns who used to drag his opponents over the goal line. I remember watching a game in the early 1960s in which he literally dragged five opponents into the end zone. Like Jim Brown, President Trump is a winner and record setter who often has to drag democrats *and* republicans across the political goal line kicking and screaming.

Respecting the office of the Presidency

A citizen of our country does not have to like or be enamored with a particular president, but all of us should respect the office. Using myself as an example, I had great disdain for presidents Johnson, Clinton, and Obama, but I have always held the office of the presidency in the highest of esteem. Though I thought President Jimmy Carter was a failure who did the best he could, I did not hold him in contempt. To me, he was someone to be pitied. In some ways, that was my guttural reaction to President Nixon. It seemed he thoroughly enjoyed being president, but too bad he had such a character flaw. Still, the office of the presidency should be held in the highest of regards. No president or any of the rest of us are perfect, because we have all sinned and come short of the glory of God.

<u>Athletes Who Insult the President</u>

President Trump usually invites successful championship sports teams to the White House, but it is amazing how many team members refuse to go. Since Trump was elected, many athletes abstained from the White House trip, they say, because of our president. To begin with, the White House is the Peoples' House, and the occupant of our House would not stop me from me from an opportunity to visit, especially by invitation. Since these Americans are athletes, I can understand their ignorance, lack of decorum, and petulant behavior, but that should not be an excuse to act like an immature child. As an example, the 2018 Major League Baseball World Series Champions the Boston Red Sox were invited to go to the White House, and the president lauded them regarding their performance on the field, "Each Red Sox player is a shining example of excellence living out the American sporting tradition that goes back many generations. . . . Right fielder J.D. Martinez thanked Trump for his hospitality, joked with the president about being a Yankee fan, and presented him with a commemorative jersey bearing the president's last name."[6] That was good, but the manager, Alex Cora, and about a dozen other players did not attend.[7] This is disgraceful and hurtful to the president. He was just trying to do a good thing in recognizing them for being the best in baseball in 2018, which is no easy task.

Another example, is the recent Super Bowl win by the New England Patriots. "While champion sports teams making a visit to the White House has long since become an annual tradition, a newer one has emerged since President Trump took office: athletes following up a title-winning performance by declaring that they'll skip the trip. . . . Brady did not visit the White House [2017] but indicated it was for family-related reasons. Other members of the team [2019], though, stated they were skipping it for political reasons."[8] That does not seem to be a mature rationale for snubbing the President of the United States. It just proves that these mentally challenged, overpaid, spoiled brutes have little to no appreciation for their good fortune. From the time they were just children, they have been treated like royalty. As a result, they have no conception of how the typical American deals with his or her daily problems. It has become so costly to attend a professional sports game, that only the wealthy have access.

Then, there is the NBA which has ceremoniously dissed the president by refusing to go to the White House. The Golden State Warriors and Toronto Raptors have made it clear they have their differences with the president to the point they are not interested in a visit to the White House. Danny Green of the 2019 NBA Champion Toronto Raptors made it clear, "It's a hard no."[9] These people need some lessons in civility and protocol. It's interesting to note, but these "hotshots" should take some lessons from the children who won the Little League World Series in 2019. The Eastbank All-Stars from River Ridge, Louisiana were victorious and they don't seem to have a problem visiting the White House.[10] The same is true of the girls from Rowan County, North Carolina who won the Little League softball World Series on August 14, 2019, they too, are thrilled to get this opportunity.[11] Perhaps, the ungrateful professionals in sports might want to model after these youngsters.

Hopefully, for the future, President Trump will reconsider inviting these so-called professionals to the White House. By the time these exorbitantly-paid professional sports figures like those previously mentioned have "made it", they have become so self-absorbed and ego-centric that they don't serve such a high honor. Invite young people of stature who have excelled in their sports. The probability is great that they will genuinely be honored by an invitation to the White House and truly appreciate the experience.

<u>What About Celebrities, News/Opinion Hosts, Politicians, and Reporters?</u>

Collectively, and in some cases, individually, some celebrities are a disgrace to the nation. Since I feel confident only intelligent people will read this book, I will not waste your time going over ludicrous, crude, and vulgar comments made by such unhinged people like Robert De Niro, Bette Midler, Sean Penn, Joy Behar, Cher, Alec Baldwin, Whoopi Goldberg and Ashley Judd—just to mention a few—who have made some of the most disgusting and disrespectful public remarks about President Trump one can imagine. It's as though they don't see him as a human being. It's worth noting that most of the aforementioned are washed up actors or singers, and I must admit, some of them I used to admire as experts at their craft. I had no idea how ignorant and insignificant they are as Americans.

Some of the "news" and opinion hosts are so sardonic and bellicose to the point of being insulting to viewers. All of the hosts on MSNBC and CNN are beyond absurd. Don Lemmon, Rachel Maddow, Joe Scarboro, Mika Brzezinski, and Anderson Cooper to mention only a few, because I cannot countenance the insanity of those inane, untalented people who have nothing good to say about President Trump. According to the old adage, "Even a broken clock is right twice a day." However, none of them ever think President Trump is ever right about anything at any time. Fox News has its foibles as well. People like Juan Williams, Chris Wallace, Neil Cavuto, Shep Smith, and others are more subtle and not as overtly insulting to President Trump. Fox began a gradual turn to the left about four years ago. After the Murdoch family took over, that network has seemed to be preparing for a CNN downward spiral as they distance themselves from President Trump.[12] People are turning to other sources such as One America News and Newsmax TV. When a vacuum occurs, it is usually filled, and perhaps it's time for a Fox replacement.

Politicians seem to have lost all sense of decorum and civility when it comes to the president. It seems they will say just about anything when invoking the name of Trump. The name is usually preceded by an expletive unfitting of an elected official, but that does not appear to cause any hesitation. In some ways, this is true of reporters because they often misbehave like out of control children who are given to yelling at and interrupting the president in midsentence. The poster-child for this disrespectful behavior is chief White House correspondent for CNN Abilo James Acosta (Jim Acosta). In June of 2019, Jim Acosta displayed his embarrassing behavior at a press conference in Osaka, Japan.[13] A short time before that, many Americans watched him make a complete fool of himself on television while trying to wrestle a microphone from a White House intern at a press conference in which the president addressed the gaggle. This is speculation, but I think the president wanted to step down from the podium and physically confront Acosta. The president stepped back from the podium, turned and walked a few steps away before returning to the presser. It appears as though he needed to collect himself which is completely understandable. President Trump, at least for now, has solved this problem. He no longer subjects press secretaries to mistreatment by White House correspondents in pressers. He handles the pressers himself without giving camera face-time to "reporters" like Jim Acosta. He answers questions on the fly, often as he is proceeding to Marine One for a flight to take care of the nation's business.

In the final analysis, after all the opposition with which the president has been faced over nearly three years, the American people should know where they want to go, and it should not be toward socialism, communism, or lawlessness. At some point, the absence of justice we see in America must be corrected, and it will take a person of great strength and determination for this to be accomplished. Thus far, President Trump has presided over a roaring economy for which he certainly should be given credit. He also made a lot of promises during the 2016 campaign. It's time to examine his major promises made and promises kept.

Promises

- Tax Cut – the American people did receive a significant tax cut, and the president has stated that another one should follow.
- Regulation Rollback – regulations have been significantly reduced with the requirement that any new regulation will have to be reduced by two still in existence. In other words, it is a 2:1 reduction ratio.
- A U.S.-Mexico Border Wall – of a 2,000-mile border, apparently, only 700 miles need a wall/barrier. By the time of the 2020 election occurs, there should be approximately 330 miles of wall/barrier in place.[14] However, the president

insists that it will be closer to 500 miles. The entire project would have been completed at least a year ago if the democrat led Congress, media, and federal courts had not stood in staunch opposition to securing the border and protecting American citizens.

- NAFTA – withdrawal from this dastardly North American Free Trade Agreement which has economically sucked this country dry. The president withdrew the USA from this agreement and has replaced it with the USMCA which is the U.S.-Mexico-Canada Agreement. At the time of this writing, the democrat led Congress has not brought this up for ratification. This is another promise kept.

- TPP – the Trans-Pacific-Partnership would have been disastrous to our trade deficits and auto industry, but the president withdrew the USA from it. Promise kept.

- Paris Climate Accord – another global-warming/climate-change bunch of liberal drivel to which Obama committed the USA, but President Trump withdrew America from this job-and-economy-killing boondoggle. Promise kept.

- Iranian Nuclear "Deal"-a deal for whom? It certainly wasn't in the best interest of the United States and the rest of the world, especially Israel.

- ObamaCare ACA Repeal – this promise was only partially kept because of Senator John McCain, who at the last minute, voted to NOT repeal this health care albatross; however, the Individual Mandate was finally stricken from the ACA in the tax reduction bill.

- Energy Independence – was achieved after about two years of Trump's presidency. He promised to open pipelines, drill for more oil, open coal mines, and he did all of that and more—promise kept.

- Pro-life – he promised to oppose abortion within existing law, and he has kept that commitment, especially late term abortions.

- Restructure of the Veterans Administration – that was accomplished through the VA Accountability Act which, according to President Trump, makes it possible for anyone who steals from or causes harm to a veteran to be fired on the spot. In addition, now if a veteran cannot obtain a timely medical appointment, they can get medical assistance from civilian providers and the federal government will pay the bill.

- Drug Pricing Reform – big Pharma has made significant reductions in the cost of needed drugs which is another promise kept.
- America First – was promised in rally after rally, which means that the interests of America supersede those of all other nations. His actions speak for themselves. One of the ways in which he has demonstrated that is his firm stance on China's intellectual theft and massive trade deficits. He not only has "drawn a line in the sand", he has poured a concrete footer deep and wide. The President is negotiating, not bloviating. The same can be said regarding the dues of the North Atlantic Treaty Organization (NATO). President Trump confronted the leaders of NATO in Europe and told them they need to start paying the original amount upon which they had previously agreed. As a result, to date, they have paid an additional $100 billion in dues! Before that, the U.S. just picked up the tab and paid the check.
- Federal Judges-appointment and confirmation of 150 federal judges with more on the way, including two Supreme Court justices, which candidate Trump promised during the 2016 campaign. Another promise kept.

<u>Effect of Ancillary Trump Influences and actions</u>

- Citizen Optimism – has returned to the nation. The American people have greater confidence in the wealth and health of the country. In general, the populace is no longer sour and dour about the future.
- The Stock Market – has set many, many all-time highs since the president's election. Individual and corporate investment has gone up significantly.
- Permanently Disabled Veterans Student Loan Forgiveness – another way for the president to show his commitment to veterans. "The debt of these disabled veterans

will be completely erased. . . . That's hundreds of millions of dollars of student loans debt for our disabled that will be completely erased."[15] Trump said.

- Food Stamps-More than 6.2 million are no longer on food stamps, which is the opposite of what the Obama administration did. It added millions and the Trump administration has gone in a very different direction which is good for the taxpayer and those dependent upon the federal government. They need their independence.

- Criminal Justice Reform – Though this issue has historically been in the democrat wheelhouse, successful passage of this legislation was spearheaded by Trump. Even CNN commentator Van Jones gave him credit. Of course, the Democrat Party operatives and media moguls ignored the president's efforts.

- Trump promised in rallies all over the USA to make America *safe* again – which he has done everything he can without the assistance of Congress and the liberal federal courts. Gangs such as MS-13 and others have been removed from the nation by the thousands and internal deportations by ICE has made a significant difference in removing U.S. lawbreaking criminals.

- Trump promised to make America *wealthy* again – and that he has done. The stock market and individual 401k's are doing exceedingly well and the economy as a whole is booming.

- Trump promised to make America *strong* again – which he has been doing by rebuilding the U.S. military in all aspects. Two budgets of more than $700 billion each has been passed and used to beef up/add to the U.S. numbers of ships, airplanes, and other sophisticated armament.

- Trump promised to eliminate ISIS – that has been done and rather quickly at that. The previous president played pattycake with ISIS fighters and was totally feckless. ISIS no longer has their beloved caliphate.

- Bring Troops Home – has been a promise which is still in progress. He has been gradually drawing down troop levels in the Middle East,[16] but he cannot do something as stupid as Obama and bring nearly all the troops home immediately without doing it properly. A responsible commander-in-chief cannot put troops who are left on the ground at an obvious disadvantage. This promise is still in progress. This is probably one of the disagreements he had with his National Security Adviser John Bolton, and that is one of the reasons they parted ways. John Bolton has been more hawkish than the president, and the president wants the U.S. withdrawn from foreign wars. President Trump appears to be more interested in peace than war. Yet, on 9/11 of 2019, the commander-in-chief had the military deliver a crushing blow to what was left of ISIS. They dropped 80,000 pounds of bombs on ISIS Island.

- Space Force – this is a necessary addition to our defense capability. Although his detractors impugn this move, they are grievously mistaken. I remember when President Reagan created the visual image of "Star Wars" which was essentially the final nail in the coffin of the old Soviet Union. The president is aware of how important this initiative is relative to cyber security. He knows that China has already well-positioned itself as the new super space force. We are well-behind, and it's not good that Communist China is leading the way.

- Mission Mars – is an important move for our space program, because it will involve the private sector as well as the National Aeronautical Space Administration (NASA). There are many things in use today because of the space program which took us to the moon. Estimates of between 1,500-1,800 spinoffs have been developed for the betterment of humankind. Even things such as the Cochlear implant for the hearing impaired, artificial limbs, and body cooling systems, just to mention a few. By the way, the space program should not be credited with the development of Tang, Teflon, or Velcro—that's just mythology. I recall watching President John F. Kennedy proclaim on television that the USA would put a man on the moon before the 1960's decade would end. Though he was murdered before the USA made it happen on July 20, 1969, his vision became a reality. What was done to NASA by Barack Hussein Obama is beyond disgraceful. That incredible agency was placed on the sidelines without mission. How despicable!

What has been listed thus far is not all inclusive. President Trump has done things for the citizens of this country only he and they know about. He is a kind and generous man who loves America. He really is a one-of-a-kind president. There are issues which need attention with which he will have to deal in the future in order to keep America great. Some of them are listed below.

Critical Future Challenges

There are significant challenges with which this country must soon come to grips. When President Trump came into office, this country was literally on the ropes financially, politically, and culturally. He has been in a triage environment since taking office and he has made many very tough calls and critical decisions.

Financial Solvency – is the debt free condition of a country wherein it can make positive investments into its future. This nation is currently operating under the weight and burden of a debt which will soon hit $23 trillion; however, that number is modest as compared to the $200 trillion in unfunded liabilities for which the federal government is responsible. In other words, We the People of the USA have this obligation.

It's easy to blame past Congresses and presidents for this crushing debt, but the reason for it is far more nefarious. According to a 1996 BBC documentary, this all began in the 1700s by the creation of private banks on the order of the Federal Reserve of the U.S., which is a private bank and has nothing to do with being a part of the federal government. That technique was used in England more than once as well as the USA. The American Federal Reserve private bank which is located in the U.S. came into being in 1913 in St. Simons Island, Georgia. It was created by northern bankers who thought they knew what was best for the citizens of America. Information about the BBC documentary can be found on utube. com/TheMoneyMasters1996FullDocumentary.[17] I hasten to add, this source was discovered because of my dear friend, Bert Hurrass, to whom I owe a debt of gratitude. If it were in my power, every high school and college student would have to become familiar with the information in the film and be able to discuss it in detail. This work is what real education should be about.

One of the erudite discoveries found in the film is the influence of the Rothschild banking family until this day upon western civilization, including the U.S. "The real power behind the United States is the Rothschild banking family, which can trace its roots to 1743 when Moses Amschel Bauer put the red hexagram above his doorway. . . . That was also the year his son Mayer was born in Bavaria. In 1760 Mayer would change the family name from Bauer to Rothschild after that red hexagram sign (Rot is German for "red" and Schild means 'sign')."[18] This is a banking family of German Jews.

The point of the previous discussion is to bring an awareness to the dangers of private banks of nations. These so-called banks don't even have reserves, and the historical study of this practice of establishing these interest charging banks quickly reveals how debt enslaves citizens of nations. That's the primary reason that President Andrew Jackson (1829-1837) did his best to eliminate the private bank of his day. The fact is the USA has not had zero debt since he was president. "Jackson's spending controls along with increased revenue enabled him to pay off the national debt in 1835 and keep the nation debt free for the remainder of his term. This is the only time in the nation's history that the federal government was debt free,"[19] and that was during President Jackson's second term. This is worth repeating. <u>This is the only time in the nation's history that the federal government was debt free</u>.

As he should be, President Trump is quite proud of his many records as president. Though it's highly unlikely that he will ever be able to match President Jackson's record regarding debt, it would certainly be an honorable goal. President Trump seems to emulate President Jackson in many ways, and Jackson did all he could to see that the private bank of his day operated without foreign investors. Hopefully, the current president will do what he can to eliminate the Fed which is a scourge upon the nation. A nation is little different than an individual when it comes to indebtedness. The main one of course is a nation can just print more money but individuals can't. This nation has done enough of that over the past decade, and it can't really afford to keep it up. This must stop. Spending must stop. The nation's credit cards are maxed out. It is impossible for a nation to spend itself into prosperity.

Over the past several years, hardly an elected official on either side of the aisle has even mentioned the debt. There was a time when republicans recoiled at the suggestion of raising the debt ceiling; however, it's now expected. Since 1917, because of WW I, the debt ceiling was created and has been raised more than 100 times since, and in 2017, 100 years later, President Trump said, "For many years people have been talking about getting rid of the debt ceiling altogether. There are lots of good reasons to do that."[20] There may be good reasons to do it, but that does not excuse the massive debt of the U.S. The nation needs to return to the thinking of President Jackson. What America needs is the elimination of the Fed and the creation of a private bank owned by the citizens of the United States without influence from foreign investors. Hopefully, the president will soon begin to turn the ship of state toward a debt-free port of call.

<u>Political Enigma</u>

President Trump is fully aware that there is a struggle for the soul of America being waged by delusional democrat socialists and Muslims. All one has to do is listen to the democrat primary candidates. What they say they believe has practically no relationship with what this nation has been historically. They speak of socialism or even communism and that is not what the Founders created or intended. Socialism or communism is tyrannical by nature; whereas, conservative republicans fully embrace liberty, freedom, and the joyful pursuit of happiness. The message of these delusional democrats is doom and gloom, that is, the sky is falling because we humans are destroying the Earth. Such poppycock! The Muslim Brotherhood now has great influence in the United States, and their goal is to rule the Earth at all costs. Over the past decade, anti-America Muslims have made great inroads into the destruction of America. They are even getting elected to the Congress and other public offices.

The prospect for bi-partisan governance is highly improbable. The parties approach the issues from opposite ends of the spectrum.

Conservative republicans believe in self-reliance, not in a bloated federal government which promises that all things are free and that American citizens have a *right* to "free stuff." If these delusional democrats would examine the lives of the Founding Fathers, they would find this thinking to be abhorrent. The Founders created a country which stood tall, not on its knees with outstretched hands, grasping for things not earned. These men had great pride in themselves and expected others to be like-minded, not beggars. They created a small limited federal government which stayed out of the lives of the citizens. If they were here today, and looked upon what we have wrought, I highly doubt a one of them would have a dry eye out of pure heart-felt sorrow for what we have done to their glorious creation which they designed for themselves, citizens of the day, and ultimately us.

Since democrats and republicans will not be working together, it leaves but only one choice for a responsible citizen. We must vote for republicans, and hope and pray that they are true conservatives, not F-Rs (fake Republicans). This is not just for 2020, but this is for the foreseeable future. As voters, we must do some research on each candidate for whom we can cast a vote. Unfortunately, most Americans have become so busy enjoying their lives in the richness and fullness of the greatest country on Earth, they have become complacent about their civic duty. It has come time for all of us to rise to the challenge of our patriotic duty and repel this attack on our republic. We must rebuke these communists socialists, and Muslims. It's up to us to rescue this nation that we love while we still can. One of the ways we can help is to insist that term limits be placed on all elective offices as well as judicial appointments. The Founders left us a means to change the Constitution when it becomes necessary to do so—the amendment process.

<u>Term Limits</u>

The Founders never intended for men and women to remain in office for 40 years or even longer. Even though some of them had long lives, life expectancy of the citizenry of the time was 36 years. We currently have people in the House and Senate who have been serving as elected officials for 30-40 years. The men who created this great republic never thought of government as a career. It was a civic duty. This is a challenge for President Trump. When he was on the campaign trail, he said that he supported term limits. After his reelection in 2020, perhaps he can fully push this issue. It will be up to him to lead the effort for term limits. He serves for eight years and is term-limited; therefore, why shouldn't members of the House and Senate be term-limited? Some argue that the citizens have the power to limit the terms of elected officials at the ballot box. That may be true, but how has that worked out for us? I highly doubt that the Founders would have agreed to pensions and free medical care for members of the House of Representatives and the Senate.

<u>Cultural melt-down</u>

Part of the problem can be laid at the feet of a very liberal immigration practice. Legally, America adds about 700,000-1,000,000 new citizens per year. That does not include millions of illegal aliens who are a burden to the U.S. taxpayer. Some estimates are as high as 30 million illegal people are occupying this land. They overburden our educational, social, health care systems, law enforcement, and our penal systems. The president has been trying to resolve this problem and he will continue to do so, but our laws and policies need to support him in greater ways. We need sensible immigration reform. The preponderance of illegal immigrants come from Mexico and the Central America countries of Guatemala, El Salvador, and Honduras. It's important to note that they all have one thing in common—the Spanish language. This nation should end the policy of printing information in Spanish and bilingual education in public schools. It's not only costly but it's very inefficient. It's not just government but business as well which caters to people who only speak Spanish. Unless we as a nation change our behavior and public policy, these immigrants will never really be inculcated into the American culture. We hope our president will be free to pursue cultural policies more fully which embrace the American culture after 2020.

Of course, immigration is not the only culprit. The general lack of propriety in speech and overt behavior, which only a generation ago, was firmly discouraged and disallowed has left us without civility and concern about pleasing God. Our Creator cannot be pleased with his creation when He who created us do all that we can to distance ourselves from Him. The vulgar language used today in the public forum should be soundly condemned and not tolerated. Electronic violent games, movies, television, songs, and pornography on the Internet in which anything goes permeate our consciousness and devalue human life. This is not about being a prude, it's about being a responsible citizen and human being who believes in standards of decorum which emphasize decency in all things.

A compounding issue which should trouble all Americans is the preoccupation with the denial of God in our lives. Over the past few years, it seems that the Democrat Party is not only anti-American but anti-God. Has the Democrat Party become Godless? So many of their overt actions certainly seem to indicate that. At the 2012 democrat convention officials eliminated references to God when they drafted the platform. "In drafting the original platform, Democratic leaders removed references to God (and to Jerusalem as the capital of Israel). They didn't merely forget to mention God; they made a conscious decision to remove Him."[21] Another source, the *Washington Times*, stated a similar observation, "The most memorable moment of the Democratic National Convention was when the delegates denied God three times from the convention floor."[22] This is reminiscent of when Peter denied Christ three times. This is perplexing, because there is no reason to exclude God from our government. That said, there is evidence that by taking this position of estrangement from God, . . . "Democrats were hugely successful across the country by solidifying their base. In the process, they have pushed away religious voters not simply by ignoring them but by actively repelling them with accusations of bigotry and backwardness. Unless they change that, Democrats haven't got a prayer to solving their God problem."[23] On a number of occasions, they have even attempted to prevent the practice of praying before such things as the beginning of committee meetings in the House. All of us need the divine guidance of God, including and especially representatives of We the People.

———

Endnotes

1   The Political Insider (July 18, 2018) Reminder: Hypocrite Bernie Sanders Honeymooned in USSR, https://the politicalinsider.com/bernie-sanders-honeymoon-ussr/ Posobiec, Jack (May 1, 2019) Yes, There Was An Attempted Coup Against Trump [Human Events] https://humanevents.com/2019/05/01/yes-there-was-an-attempted-coup-against-trump/?utm...

2   Posobiec, Jack (May 1, 2019) Yes, There Was An Attempted Coup Against Trump [Human Events] https://humanevents.com/2019/05/01/yes-there-was-an-attempted-coup-against-trump/?utm...

3   Hunter, Greg (April 28, 2019) Trump Coup Biggest Violation of Constitution in History – Kevin Shipp [USAWatchdog™] https://usawatchdog.com/trump-coup-biggest-violation-of-constitution-in-hitory-kevin-shipp/

4   Free Republic (June 12, 2019) Italian PM Fires 2 Intel Chiefs: Working W/Brennan On Coup Attempt Against Our President [Opinion] https://www.freerepublic.com/focus/f-news/3756252

5   LAROUCHE Pac (September 20, 2018) Britain's Coup Attempt Against President Trump Is Blowing Up in Its Face – Act Now to End the Empire for Good, https://larouchepac.com/20180920/britains-coup-attempt-against-president-trump-blowing-i...

6   Uria, Daniel (May 9, 2019) MLB champion Boston Red Sox visit White House [UPI] http://www.upi.com/Top_News/US/2019/05/09/MLB-champions-Red-Sox-visit-Wh...

7   Ibid.

8   Bieler, Des (February 4, 2019) After Super Bowl win, Patriots waste no time saying they won't visit White House, *Washington Post*, https://www.washingtonpost.com/sports/2019/02/05/after-super-bowl-win-patriots-players-...

9   Delgado, Dane (June 23, 2019) Danny Green on White House visit with Donald Trump: 'It's a hard no' (VIDEO), [NBC Sports] https://nba.nbcsports.com/2019/06/23/danny-green-on-white-house-visit-with-donald-trump...

10 Foster, Kevin (August 25, 2019) La. Little League team invited to White House after shutout World Series

win [WAFB] https://www.wafb.com/2019/08/26/celebration-after-historic-little-league-world-series-win-...

11 Boren, Cindy & Bogage, Jacob (August 28, 2019) Trump invites Little League World Series softball and baseball champs to the White House, *The Washington Post*, [Sports] https://www.washingtonpost.com/sports/2019/08/26/trump-tells-louisiana-little-league-wor...

12 Data Lounge – Fox News distancing themselves from Trump and Hannity? https://datalounge.com/thread/22481399-fox-news-distancing-themselves-From-trump...

13 Hurt, Charles (June 30, 2019) Jim Acosta of CNN, an embarrassment to village idiots, *Washington Times*, https://m.washingtontimes.com/news/2019/jun/30Jim-acosta-cnn-embarrassment-village-i...

14 Fitzgerald, Sandy (August 12, 2019) Border Patrol Chief: 330 Miles of Wall Up By End of 2020 [Newsmax] https://www.newsmax.com/newsfront/provost-border-patrol-wall/2019/08/12/id/928258/

15 O'Reilly, Andrew (August 21, 2019) Trump signs executive order cancelling student loan debt for disabled veterans [Fox News] https://www.foxnews.com/Politics/trump-signs-executive-order-cancelling-student-loan-debt-for-disabled-veterans

16 Dominguez, Gabriel [London] & Cloughly, Brian [London] Trump reportedly orders major US troop drawdown from Afghanistan, *Jane's Defence Weekly*, https://www.janes.com/article/85393/trump-reportedly-orders-major-us-troop-drawdown-from-afganistan

17 The Money Masters 1996 BBC Full Documentary [utube.com/TheMoneyMasters1996FullDocumentary]

18 American History of the Rothschilds and the Eight Most Powerful Families.Humansarefree.com/2017/05/American-history-of-rothschilds.and.html

19 Andrew Jackson's Hermitage [Presidency I Andrew Jackson's Time in Office as President] https://thehermitage.com/learn/andrew-jackson/president/Presidency/

20 Hiltzik, Michael (July 16, 2019) Column: With the debt ceiling fight, Congress and Trump are playing with fire – again,

Los Angeles Times, https://www.latimes.com/business/story/2019-07-16-debt-ceiling-fight

21 Lawler, Phil (September 6, 2012) Did Democrats really boo God? Not quite. It's worse than that, [Trinity Communications] https://www.catholicculture.org/Commentary/the-city-gates.cfm?id=402

22 *Washington Times* [Analysis] (September 6, 2012) Editorial: Obama's party says no to God, https://www.washingtontimes.com/news2012/sep/6/obamas-party-says-no-to-god/

23 Zita, Salena (March 15, 2017) Democrats still haven't faced their God problem, *New York Post*, https://nypost.com/2017/03/15/democrats-still-haven't-faced-their-god-problem/

Epilogue

This has been a journey of love for God, our nation, the memory of the Founding Fathers, and our great president Donald J. Trump. I have written a number of nonfiction books on a variety of subjects, as well as fictional novels, but in my opinion, none of them are as important as this one. Though before I started this writing, as an outsider, I had a fairly good understanding of President Trump, but down my road of research, I've learned a lot more about him and the condition of our country. As I mentioned in the Prologue, I never really took him seriously until he formally became a candidate for the presidency. It was then that I knew he would become president. After watching every rally, and my other research, my admiration and respect for him as a man, phenomenon, and president, has grown exponentially. I've never seen a tougher man with such great inner strength. Put another way, I've always considered myself to be doggedly resolute, but it would take a special dispensation from God for me to be able to emulate President Trump. As a man, I could not withstand the negative forces which harangue him daily. Other than God, one of the things which seem to give him buoyancy is the high-energy level which is prevalent in every rally. His supporters let him know they are with him when he is assailed by the left and that they will stand with him no matter what.

If this man is the Devil incarnate as painted by his adversaries, how could his first wife, Ivana Trump, not see him that way? They had three children together and divorce is much like the death of a relative or someone very close. One would think she would be bitter and filled with retribution, but that is not what she penned in her 2017 book titled *Raising Trump*. Even in the dedication of the book she said, *"And to Donald, the kids' father and my dear friend."* She also reaffirmed that Donald Trump had nothing to do with drugs or alcohol. "Donald never touched a drop of alcohol or any drugs." She also discussed his involvement with the education of their children. "Parent-teacher conferences had a high priority. Donald always came to those, and usually let me do the talking." This does not sound like a self-absorbed ogre to me. Regarding her business venture, she had this to say, "I learned the business by listening to Donald—to be a tough negotiator, trust my gut, and value and reward loyalty—and the kids learned it by listening to both of us." Ivana and Donald Trump were obviously very involved with the lives of their children, and that's not indicative of parents of equivocal character. Their three children have grown up to be incredibly productive and loving parents themselves. President Trump takes great pride and joy in his relationship with his grandchildren. They are very special to him and my guess is they feel that way about him. To them, he's not Mr. President, he's just grandad.

Another thing I've learned from this sojourn is that, with the exception of We the People, he has had to stand alone, and for that I'm genuinely sorry. It is to be expected that delusional democrats will do all they can to impede his great work, because they only want *power* to the detriment of the needs of the nation. In that regard, there are far too many fake republicans (F-Rs) who are Judas in nature. What kind of people are they? How can they be so dishonest, untrustworthy, duplicitous, and disloyal? How can they sleep at night? It would seem that in light of his victory in 2016 by accumulating 306 Electoral College votes no republican would want to turn their backs on him. In some cases, even after he has campaigned on their behalf, they have rejected him. Some of us don't have much, but we do have our honor.

The so-called mainstream media has given these F-Rs plenty of cover, because more than 90% of their stories have been negative about a man who works tirelessly and unselfishly for our nation. The mainstream media has colluded with the Democrat Party in the dissemination of fake narratives such as Trump being a racist, white supremacist, and xenophobe. It has promulgated fake stories about an impending recession which has no basis in fact. The media criticizes him for everything. Despite all of that, he continues to stand tall in the face of a relentless prevarication storm. President Trump is truly historic by anyone's honest measures, and he hasn't even completed the third year of his first term. The president has become the master of multitasking. How he can complete so many unrelated tasks simultaneously are a mystery. At a distance, I watch this man perform as though he is a great conductor, standing in front of the most accomplished orchestra in the history of the world, or the Ringmaster in a circus in the greatest show on Earth. A great conservative radio host, James T. Harris, out of Phoenix, Arizona has a show called the Conservative Circus, and he proudly proclaims to be the Ringmaster, and he is an entertaining and terrific persona, but President Trump's antics would challenge him or anyone, and my guess is he would agree. Speaking of great patriotic conservative voices, let me list some of them I have been listening to intently for quite some time, especially in the writing and researching of this book.

- Rush Hudson Limbaugh III – is the "big voice" on the right who has an estimated 20 million radio listeners nationwide who began his nationally syndicated show in 1988. He is also an author of both adult and children's books. He is the Godfather of talk radio and syndicated on 600 stations nationwide.
- Mark Levin – is one of the brightest conservative personalities on television and radio. He is a Constitutional scholar with passion. His new book, *Unfreedom of the Press* is superb. I have learned much from Levin's CRTV program. His guests are usually outstanding relative to being educational.
- Lou Dobbs – is a patriotic conservative who is heard on the Salem Radio Network coast to coast. Dobbs has the best show on Fox business called Lou Dobbs Tonight, which is comprised of great opinion and discussion relative to world and U.S. issues. He is very supportive of President Trump. His show is number one on Fox Business. He is one of the most passionate personalities on air.
- Sean Hannity – is a conservative radio and television personality of notoriety and popularity who is an influential registered Conservative. Hannity has supported President Trump 100% from the very beginning.
- Mike Gallagher – of the Mike Gallagher Show is a true patriot conservative radio host who does a lot of charity work. He is nationally syndicated and supports President Trump 100%.
- Larry Elder – of The Larry Elder Show is an incredibly bright conservative radio host who is able to analyze and deal with

complex issues rapidly. He is known as The Sage from South Central.

- Mark Steyn – is a highly intelligent citizen of Canada and successful author who provides terrific humor at SteynOnline.com. His insights, opinions, and observations are humorous and enlightening. With some frequency, he guest-hosts Rush Limbaugh's radio show, as well as appearing on a number of Fox News and opinion shows from time to time.

Those listed above are not all inclusive, but they have been most important in my research. Notice, I did not waste my time with mindless delusional liberals who are only blocks away from a mental institution. I value my life and time too much to squander both.

On September 16, 2019 President Trump held a rally in Rio Rancho, New Mexico in which he connected with a huge crowd in his inimitable way. Before the president arrived, I watched people in line being interviewed hours before the event officially began. That is an education in and of itself and another reason I prefer Right Side Broadcasting. Many Hispanics talked about the greatness of the president and that they wanted to hear more about stopping illegal immigration and the promised wall. The female Hispanics wearing Trump paraphernalia which had "Women for Trump" emblazoned on their shirts and blouses were proud of their support. Interestingly, there were quite a number of very young supporters who were eager to see and hear the president. As is my custom, I watched the rally online, and since this is the last rally, I will be able to vicariously attend before this book goes to press, it is important to recount some of his message and speech. A central theme was energy independence and the role of New Mexico. He stressed that this nation is number one in energy dominance throughout the world and that the USA is a net exporter of energy. Trump spoke of his support for clean water and air, and he also reminded the thousands of his supporters at the rally that China, Russia, India, and other countries are polluting the environment at will, because none of those nations are being held to the same standards as the U.S. He reminded everyone that 6,000,000 new jobs have been added to the U.S. economy since his election. The president also stressed that his pro-growth, pro-jobs, and pro-America strategy with emphasis on *America first*, is a winner! He also proclaimed that, unlike 2016, he would win New Mexico in 2020. Though the state only has five electoral votes, the president wants to win every state and electoral vote.

During his speech, he mentioned that New Mexico now has a one-billion dollar surplus, and added, "Thank you President Trump," he said humorously, because the state has been the beneficiary of dramatic energy increases, and he quickly added that the democrats want to bankrupt the state by killing its energy production. He also pointed out that wages in the state are growing at 3% and is experiencing a nearly 30% growth rate in new business applications. New Mexico is leading the nation, and looking at the rate of growth in business applications as compared to the other 49 states, that is impressive. It's very difficult to gauge the number of Hispanics who were present at the rally, but it looked and sounded like about 30%. The president also mentioned that since his election Hispanic wages have increased by 8%. Some other issues about which he spoke dealt with giving power back to the people and the need to get the replacement trade agreement (USMCA) ratified by the democrat led Congress. He also made a special point regarding the democrat body of commissioners who have been complaining to Washington, D.C. about their inability to absorb the numbers of illegal aliens in their communities. He reintroduced humor by poking fun at our "Paper Mache" automobiles. He was of the opinion that they are too light and not safe enough. He also joked about our light bulbs. The president said that we are going to be able to purchase incandescent (regular) light bulbs again, rather than those dangerous, gas filled, and costly bulbs we now have to use. He did not mention how we ended up with these mostly Chinese manufactured bulbs, but this happened during the reign of horror of the Obama administration.

This rally was much like all of the rest. It was high-energy and filled with excitement. The attendees were raucous yet respectful. They came to have fun and get an opportunity to see President Trump. Many of them had waited in line for more than five hours. They were given to shouting familiar themes such as "USA, USA, USA! And Build the Wall!" There were only two people in attendance who were not there for good reasons. One was removed near the beginning of the president's speech and one just before the end. The president joked about what the media would say the next day,

"Protesters Erupt At Trump Rally!" He then laughed and joked about the "lame stream media" and fake news. With some frequency, he also tells a story about someone he knows who is very wealthy but doesn't like him, and according to the president, the feelings are mutual. He said one day he encountered this man at the White House, and asked, "What are *you* doing here?" His answer was very telling," You're doing quite a job, and I don't have any choice but to vote for you." At the Rally in Rio Rancho, New Mexico, that is what he said to the crowd. He told them that even if they don't like him, they have to vote for him. In reality he is correct, because any and all of those delusional democrats are saying things which are unrealistic and are sounding as though they have mental issues.

It was September 18, 2019 when Rush Limbaugh on his radio show provided an excellent analysis on the democrat attempt to impeach Associate Justice Brett Kavanaugh. Many Americans watched on television as the Democrat "debacle" Party tried to prevent him from becoming a justice on the Supreme Court. They did all they could to discredit and destroy this man and his family, but they failed miserably, and he was confirmed. Mr. Limbaugh opines that the reason the Democrat Party is now trying to impeach Kavanaugh is because they are losing control of the Court, and the president is remaking the federal court system upon which they have relied for decades, and now even the makeup of the historically rogue 9th Circuit Court is changing. President Trump has already made 150 lifetime appointments which have been confirmed. According to the president, he expects to appoint another 30 federal judges, bringing the total to 180. This is obviously the Democrat Party's greatest fear, because the actions of President Trump now will have an effect on the legal system for generations to come which will slow the socialist democrats from progressing to their ultimate destruction of the America which the Founders created.

Another thing which has caused the delusional Democrat Party trepidation is the prospect that President Trump cannot be defeated in 2020. As a result of that Trump phobia, on September 24, 2019, Nancy Pelosi, as Speaker of the House, called a press conference to announce that the Congress was going to conduct a formal Impeachment Inquiry regarding a conversation President Trump had with President Volodymyr Zelenskiy of Ukraine July 25, 2019.

According to the assertion of crazed democrats, President Trump had pressured President Zelenskiy to investigate former Vice President Joe Biden and his son Hunter for exactly what they were accusing President Trump of doing. In response to this absolute fabrication, President Trump released the entire telephone conversation he had with President Zelenskiy on September 25, 2019, and clearly President Trump did nothing wrong. Once again these mentally disturbed democrats came up with filthy, fatuous, vacuous hands. To show how desperate these crackbrain democrats have become, Congressman Al Green said that if they don't impeach Trump, he will be reelected. That statement says it all, that is, if they can't stop the president now through impeachment, the people will return him to office. In other words, democrats want to prevent the will of the people from becoming a reality.

Despite the insanity of the Democrat Party, we Americans should be thankful to God that we were born or naturalized in the United States of America. I feel very privileged to live in this land and enjoy the fruits of its liberty and freedom. Though like many Americans, I have travelled a great deal outside of this magnificent country, but I have never been anywhere I would even *consider* trading for the United States of America—thanks be to God!

President Donald J. Trump 2020!

———

Index